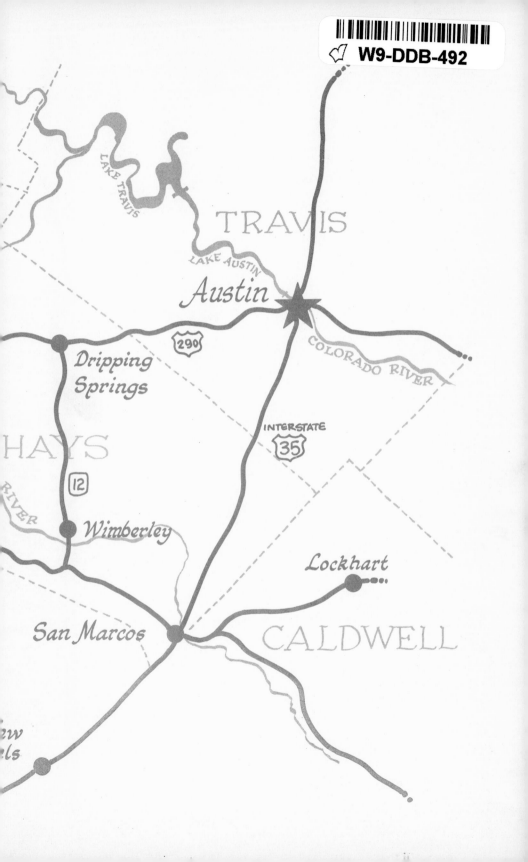

Lyndon Baines Johnson

THE FORMATIVE YEARS

Lyndon Baines Johnson

The Formative Years

WILLIAM C. POOL

EMMIE CRADDOCK

DAVID E. CONRAD

Illustrated by Boyd Saunders

SAN MARCOS

Southwest Texas State College Press

1965

Printed for

SOUTHWEST TEXAS STATE COLLEGE

by Von Boeckmann-Jones Press

AUSTIN, TEXAS

PREFACE

The story that follows is an account of the Texas hill country; the people who pioneered the land only a few short decades ago; and the forces, both human and physical, that shaped the destiny of young Lyndon Baines Johnson, a child of the brush-covered hills that form the rimland of the Great Plains of western America. Early in 1964 the late John G. Flowers, then president of Southwest Texas State College, suggested that there was a need for such a work and projected the original plan upon which this study of Johnson's formative years is based.

As is true with all historical monographs, this book is the product of the labor of various people. In giving credit to whom credit is due, our obligations are many, but several merit special mention: Rebekah Johnson Bobbitt of Austin, who opened her home and made her family scrapbook and records available; the late J. R. Buckner, professor of modern languages at Southwest Texas State, who spent several days in travel about the region of Gillespie and Blanco counties in search of source materials; Ava Johnson Cox of Johnson City, who took time from a busy schedule to recount stories of a happy childhood along the Pedernales; Willard Deason, Jesse Kellam, and Dr. Alfred H. Nolle, former dean of the college, whose recollections contributed materially to the reconstruction of his college days; Helen Weinberg, colleague of Johnson at Sam Houston high school and respected teacher of history in the Houston public schools until her recent retirement, who gave generously of her time and knowledge and through whom other valuable sources were made available; and Welly H. Hopkins of Washington, D. C., senior counsel for the United Mine Workers of America, whose account of his political association in 1930 and 1931 with the future President, comprises a significant chapter in this book.

To numerous others, many of whom are cited in the pages that follow, we are deeply indebted. Particular thanks are due Dorothea Bright Askew of Houston, whose memory of Johnson as a young man added much to the development of this narrative;

L. E. Jones, Jr. of Corpus Christi, star debater at Sam Houston in 1930-31, who provided excellent materials concerning Johnson's teaching career; Kitty McLaughlin and Paul Cotulla for arranging interviews with former colleagues and students of the President in Cotulla; the late John G. Flowers; James H. Mc-Crocklin, president of Southwest Texas State College; and Leland E. Derrick, dean of graduate studies, who served as coordinator of the project.

Finally, we would like to express our appreciation to Beverly Conrad, Merry FitzPatrick, Barry Bascom Hayes, Hennie Pinkston, Everette Swinney, and Sarah Jeannette Pool who assisted in the detailed tasks of preparing the manuscript for publication.

September, 1965

William C. Pool
Emmie Craddock
David E. Conrad

CONTENTS

Lyndon Baines Johnson

The Formative Years

For Susan and Bill,
with all good wishes,

Emmie Craddock

David E Conrad

William C Pool

I.

THE LAND AND THE PEOPLE

1

SINCE THE DAY OF THOMAS JEFFERSON, A CHILD OF THE VIRGINIA backcountry, the American people have displayed a curious interest in the geographical environment and the historical background of local regions that produce presidents of the United States; this curiosity is even more acute when the man in question originates in humble circumstances and climbs the political ladder to the highest office of the land.

In a speech nominating Lyndon Baines Johnson at the 1964 Democratic National Convention, Governor John Connally of Texas explained to his nation-wide audience that "the Hill Country of Texas is a stern adversary, giving grudgingly of itself only to the most determined. It is a land that weaves strong resilient human fiber, conditioned to adversity, grateful for good fortune. This is the native land of Lyndon Baines Johnson. . . . Here at the grass roots of America, where the soil is meager and the sun is hot, he learned about life and about people."[1] A few months

---

[1]Austin *American,* August 27, 1964.

before, George Silk and the staff writers of one of the popular national weekly magazines, visiting the Texas Hill Country in the dead of winter, remarked that when winter comes "the sky, stretched horizon to far horizon, turns shockingly blue. Cold bites the leaves but the blazing sun splashes gold upon the land. The Spanish oak and sumac flame red, and giant pecans shake down their tender nuts. Angora goats and sheep turn their rumps to the north and graze on. The raccoons come out, wild turkey cry in the brush, armadillos shuffle by. Fifty deer graze at once on a winter oat field—and at a sudden noise clear the fence like arrows loosed from 50 bows. . . . This land is like no other part of the state. It is a land of little hills and valleys, of limestone springs and cedar and live oak trees that stay green all year. It is gentle but deceptive, for it knows heat that darkens stone, drought that wilts even cactus [prickly pear], floods that sweep a valley clean. Because it is harsh, it tested the men who settled it."[2] These examples represent excellent and accurate efforts by two persons— a politician-statesman and a journalist—to describe the natural beauty and harshness of the region of Southwest Texas known to the natives as simply the "Hill Country."

It is apparent that both Governor Connally and George Silk realized the significance of a lesson well learned by native historians and geographers of Texas and the Southwest—that a complete understanding of the relationship between an environment and the civilization resting upon it is dependent, in turn, on knowledge of the geology, topography, plant life, and animal life of the region. If the nature of the land determines, to a great extent, the composite character of the people who reside upon it, then it is proper to begin the story of the formative years of Lyndon Baines Johnson, his frontier ancestors, and his contemporary neighbors with a geographical and historical description of the Texas Hill Country, truly a land of great scenic beauty which has presented a significant challenge to the families that have occupied it.

2

Geographers and historians extend and continue the Great Plains region southward from the High Plains of West Texas and

<hr>

[2] *Life*, February 14, 1964.

New Mexico to the Rio Grande and beyond to the line of the Balcones Escarpment; it is this extension of the Great Plains that forms the Edwards Plateau—a geographical area bounded on the south by the Rio Grande, on the north by the Colorado River, on the west by the Pecos River and the Stockton Plateau, and on the east by the Balcones fault line. Extending in a curved line from Del Rio on the Rio Grande to the Red River, the Balcones Escarpment is visible from Del Rio to the vicinity of Austin as a range of wooded hills separating the Edwards Plateau from the coastal plains to the south and east. Throughout its entire course from the Rio Grande to the Colorado River, the Balcones fault is a single, definite geological feature—one of the most distinctive in Texas. The accompanying hills "have the appearance of balconies when viewed from the plain below and this undoubtedly accounts for the Spanish name, *balcones.*"[3]

To the geologist, the rugged, well-dissected limestone plain immediately west of the Balcones fault represents an erosional region in which a thin soil covers beveled Comanche limestone exposures which extend northward to form the bedrock underpinning of the High Plains. In semi-technical language, the Edwards limestone lies above the Permian and Triassic beds and beneath the more recent Pliocene and Pleistocene deposits (the latter forming the surface of the High Plains). As indicated, the Edwards, or Comanche, limestone region has suffered heavily from erosion of the ages; and any loose soil-blanket that might have once covered the surface has long since been carried away.[4]

Actually the true Hill Country of Texas comprises only the frayed and dissected eastern margins of the larger Edwards Plateau. This eastern rimland is characterized by ranges of rugged hills and by the numerous canyons of the streams that rise in the interior of the tableland and flow southeastward through the Balcones fault as they continue on their way to the Gulf of Mexico. The most notable of these spring-fed, cypress-and-pecan-bordered watercourses include the Nueces, Frio, Medina, Guadalupe, Blanco, and Pedernales rivers; and of these, only the Blanco and the Pedernales are important to our story. The Blanco

---

[3] *Texas Almanac,* 1961-1962, p. 45; Walter P. Webb and H. Bailey Carroll (eds.), *The Handbook of Texas,* I, 102 (hereafter cited as *Handbook of Texas*).

[4] *Texas Almanac,* 1961-1962, 105.

and Pedernales rivers, with numerous small tributaries—also often spring-fed—drain an area of the Hill Country comprised within the borders of Gillespie, Kendall, Blanco, and Hays counties.

Since the land along the Pedernales River valley near the Blanco-Gillespie County line provides the natural setting of the two counties, the southwest historian turns, as he often does, to the *Handbook of Texas*. Writing about her native Blanco County for the *Handbook,* Bessie Brigham reports:

The surface [of the county] is largely hilly to mountainous and ranges from woody, rocky lands to fertile soil. The timber sections include cedar, cypress, mesquite, white oak, walnut, pecan, and hickory. Since deer and wild turkey have always been abundant and the rivers offer excellent facilities for camping and fishing, Blanco County has long been among the recreational centers of the state. The altitude ranges from 720 to 1600 feet, the annual rainfall is 29.51 inches, and the mean temperature is 65.4 degrees. . . .

The leading industries are the production of wool and mohair and the raising of beef cattle, with dairying and poultry on the increase. Crops include grain, corn, sorghum, tomatoes, peaches, pecans, honey, and a wide variety of fruit and vegetables. Hunting leases in the county yield $120,000 annual income. . . .

Reporting on Gillespie County to the west, Julia Estill writes:

Gillespie County with an altitude of 1000 to 2100 feet, lies in the broken, largely wooded Edwards Plateau of Southwest Texas drained by the Pedernales River. The average rainfall is twenty-six to twenty-eight inches; the mean temperature is 65.5 degrees. Black soil and sandy loams predominate, the upland timbers being cedar, oak, blackjack, and mesquite; along streams grow elm, cottonwood, willow, and pecan. Limestone and fine-grain red granite are quarried for commercial purposes. . . . The main crops in cultivation are small grain, corn, grain sorghums, some cotton, peanuts, vegetables, and stony fruits. Little, if any, artificial irrigation is needed. Ranch lands make up 80 per cent of the county; sheep, Angora goats, cattle, hogs, horses, and mules are sources of income. Of the 1500 farms and ranches, only 4 per cent are tenant farms.[5]

Bounded by the Colorado River drainage basin on the north and the Balcones Escarpment on the east, Blanco and Gillespie counties comprise the heartland of the picturesque Texas Hill Country. Sharing all of the general characteristics of the more

---

[5]*Handbook of Texas,* I, 172, 690.

extensive Edwards Plateau, these two counties feature limestone soils, with alluvial clays and black and sandy loams predominating. This shallow soil cover supports a growth of native grasses that includes little bluestem, grama, threeawn, buffalo grass, and curly mesquite. The timber cover, sparse when compared to the forests of the eastern woodlands, consists of mountain juniper or cedar; Spanish oak; post oak; numerous live oak, both large and scrub varieties; blackjack oak; pecan; cypress; elm; and a wide variety of shrubs native to Southwest Texas. One of the most significant characteristics of the area is the dense growth of cedar found on the slopes of the hills and buttes. In fact, the cedar cover is of such importance that, in classifying the plant-life regions of Texas, the *Texas Almanac* labels the Hill Country as "the cedar brakes." The demand for cedar posts and poles has been so great in the past that the Hill Country and the lower reaches of the Western Cross Timbers have given rise to an independent, rugged individualistic class of people known locally as "cedar-choppers," an occupation group beautifully described by the late Roy Bedichek in his *Adventures of a Texas Naturalist* and pointed to by Robert H. Montgomery, professor of economics at the University of Texas, as one of the few remaining independent economic groups in America.

Of great interest to the institutional historian is the fact that the Blanco-Pedernales region of the Hill Country lies just west of the 98° meridian, labeled by Walter P. Webb as "an institutional fault (compared to a geological fault) running from the middle of Texas to Illinois or Dakota. . . . At this *fault* the ways of life and living changed. Practically every institution that was carried across it was either broken and remade or else greatly altered."[6] A close look at the climatical and rainfall statistics will give meaning to the Webb hypothesis as it is related to the Hill Country frontier. The average annual rainfall for Blanco County is approximately 29.5 inches, and for Gillespie County 28.37 inches; at the same time the mean annual temperature varies in Blanco County from 48° in January to 83° in July, with approximately the same figures applying to the Gillespie territory. Faced with borderline conditions such as these, the

---

[6] Walter P. Webb, *The Great Plains* (New York, 1935), 8.

farmers and ranchers of the region often find that the rains provide insufficient moisture for the fields and ranges. It is then that the heat-searing drouths, an intermittent feature of life on the Edwards Plateau, stalk the land, causing crops to wither and die in the fields, the live oak to shed their leaves and stand bare against the cloudless sky, the springs to cease to flow and the so-called perennial streams to dry up, and the stock ponds to shrink into flats of caked mud. The drouth brings despair, gloom, and depression to the land to dim the hopes of the sturdy agrarian folk who depend entirely on the soil for a livelihood. The farmers and ranchers sell their surplus cattle at low prices and wait in vain for "better times" or a "more seasonable year."

To compound the natural hardships of the Hill Country way of life, torrential rains not infrequently bring floods to the rapid-flowing streams of the hills; it is then that the narrow river and creek valleys are swept clean of all that stands in the way of the roaring waters—the remnants of crops, giant cypress and pecan trees, the bridges (both primitive and modern) are swept downstream. Through the ages these natural hardships have added to the already difficult task facing agricultural and ranching regions in both Texas and the nation as a whole; they have become an inseparable part of the "farm problem." Aside from the battle to overcome the obstacles of nature, the pioneers entering the Texas Hill Country during and following the 1840's and 1850's found it necessary to adapt old institutions to meet the new conditions and way of life characteristic of the American West; as a result, new methods of tilling the soil, new ways of fighting the Indian, new materials for homes and fences, and a new method of handling cattle on horseback represent only a few of the more significant adaptations demanded by the frontier.

It is also true that the nature of the land dictates, to a large extent, the choice of an occupation by the American and European pioneers who formed the vanguard of the Texas frontier. As noted in preceding paragraphs, only a small portion of the Hill Country is suited for cultivation. As the result of the absence of extensive arable land, the Edwards Plateau and Hill Country has achieved prominence as an important ranching area for Texas and the Southwest. The relatively dry climate and the nutritious grasses grown in the calcareous soils are most favorable for cattle, sheep, and goats. The first cattle were brought into Southwest Texas by the pioneer settlers, and the Texas Longhorn dominated the economy of the open range as the worthy predecessor of the blooded stock. The first Angora goats were brought into Texas by W. W. Haupt of Hays County in 1857-1858. In the years that followed, the limited number of Angoras led to cross-breeding with the slick-haired Mexican goat and the ultimate development of a "native" Angora whose fleece was marketable. Since the 1920's Texas has produced 85 per cent of the mohair clipped in the United States. Ranchers of Blanco and Gillespie counties have contributed their share to this impressive total. The first sheep were brought into Southwest Texas by the early Spanish colonists; but, in the decades after the Texas Revolution, George Wilkins Kendall was among the first to give attention to large-scale sheep ranching. As will be noted later, Kendall was then a resident of Blanco County. The primary point of interest to an area historian is that the frontiersmen who settled the land a century ago had but little latitude in their choice of an occupation; and the essential nature of the geology, the topography, the nature of the soil, and the native plant life determined the primary characteristics of the subsequent civilization that evolved in this picturesque and harsh region of Texas.

3

During the three centuries (1521-1821) that mark the Spanish colonial period in the history of Texas, the tablelands beyond the Balcones Escarpment appeared to the *conquistador* and Franciscan friar as a distant range of blue-green hills to the west of the Old San Antonio Road. Although the Spanish established a fortified mission settlement near San Pedro Springs at San Antonio de Bexar in 1718 and another, the presidio-mission San Francisco de Xaviar, near the San Marcos Springs in 1755 and sent Fernando del Bosque and Fray Juan Larios to explore the land north of present Eagle Pass as early as 1675, they founded no mission nor presidio settlement in the Edwards Plateau region until the ill-fated San Saba settlement near present Menard in 1757. The reasons for this long period of neglect are exactly two:

(1) the Lipan Apache Indians, a native race that dominated all of the western part of Texas from the Rio Grande to the Panhandle when the Spanish first came to the state, and (2) the Comanche tribes of the southern Great Plains, who later drove a wedge between the Apache and Caddo territory and terrorized both the Spanish and the later Anglo-American settlers.

When the Anglo-American frontiersmen entered Spanish-Mexican Texas after the year 1821, they, too, avoided the hill country in favor of the fertile lands of the coastal plains in general and the valleys of the Brazos, Trinity, and Colorado rivers in particular. It should be pointed out that two factors influenced the settlement of Texas: the abundant lands of the coastal plain and the fear of the wild Indians of the western plains. As a result, at the close of the Texas Revolution in the spring of 1836, the frontier line of settlement roughly followed the Old San Antonio Road from San Antonio through Bastrop and Crockett to Nacogdoches, and thence due north to the Red River near Clarksville. The lands of the Texas Hill Country remained free and unoccupied. Except for the names of the principal rivers—the Nueces, the Frio, the Medina, the Guadalupe, the Blanco, and the Colorado—the Spanish conquerors had left little imprint upon the land. Nor were the Americans ready to make an immediate move beyond the Balcones.

With the exception of the isolated and unrecorded adventures of the hunters and trappers, always the advance guard in the history of the frontier, the Anglo-American approach to the Hill Country began on June 7, 1842, when the Republic of Texas entered into a colonization contract with Henry F. Fisher and Burchard Miller to settle one thousand families of German, Swiss, Danish, Swedish, and Norwegian immigrants on a large tract of land (3,000,000 acres) lying between the Llano and Colorado rivers. Henry Fisher soon went to Germany to promote his colonization scheme. In June of 1844 he sold an interest in the Fisher-Miller contract to the Adelsverein; in December, 1845, Fisher and Miller sold all of their rights in the grant to the society.

The Adelsverein, or Association of Noblemen, also known as the Meinzer Verein, had been organized in April, 1842, by a group of German noblemen at Biebrich-on-the-Rhine for the purpose of purchasing land in the Republic of Texas. While this is neither the time nor the place to trace the activities of the Verein in detail,[7] perhaps it should be mentioned that, following a modification of the purpose of the organization at Mainz in March, 1844, when an organization was established for the protection of German immigrants in Texas, Prince Carl of Solms-Braunfels came to Texas to look after the affairs of the Association. The first German immigrants arrived at Galveston in 1844 and, after some indecision growing out of conflicts concerning the nature of land-purchase agreements, settled at New Braunfels, where Solms-Braunfels had purchased two leagues of land in March, 1845. The establishment of New Braunfels near Comal Spring at the foot of the Balcones fault in 1845 marks a significant milestone in the march toward the Hill Country of Texas.

In April, 1845, Prince Carl returned to Germany; and John O. Meusebach took over the complicated affairs of the Adelsverein. In May of 1846 Meusebach led a wagon train of some 120 settlers from New Braunfels and established Fredericksburg, four miles north of the Pedernales River on Barron's Creek. These German pioneer settlers were of many types and talents; there were skilled craftsmen, builders, traders, farmers, and professional men—all classes of European society were represented. Indian difficulties were avoided by the Meusebach-Comanche Treaty of 1847, an agreement which established a lasting peace between the German colonists and the Indians. Established as a way-station between New Braunfels and the Fisher-Miller grant, Fredericksburg grew rapidly; by the summer of 1847 the frontier village boasted eighteen stores and the Nimitz Hotel. Reinforced by the Mormon settlement at Zodiac, four miles south of Fredericksburg on the Pedernales, and the establishment of Fort Martin Scott, the German pioneers organized Gillespie County in 1848 with Fredericksburg as the county seat; the census of 1850 listed

---

[7]Readers not familiar with German colonization in Texas should consult Rudolph L. Biesele, *The History of the German Settlements in Texas, 1831-1861* (Austin, 1930); Don H. Biggers, *German Pioneers in Texas* (Fredericksburg, 1925); Ferdinand Roemer, *Texas* (Bonn, 1849; Oswald Mueller, tr., San Antonio, 1936); Viktor Bracht, *Texas in 1848* (C. F. Schmidt, tr., San Antonio, 1931); and *Pioneers in God's Hills* (Gillespie County Historical Society, 1960).

the population of the new county as 1,235; of this number, 734 lived at Fredericksburg.

Nestled snug in a green valley rimmed by evergreen hills, Fredericksburg has remained through the years a trim, clannish, thoroughly German town with an Old World flavor in architecture and in the devotion of the population to the German culture and folkways of its founders. In the years following 1846-1847, the colonists began to enjoy prosperity. The country around the Pedernales was rich in fish and game. Fertile valleys were watered by abundant streams and the wooded hills provided building stone. The thrifty settlers laid the foundations for the present prosperous region of sheep, goat, and cattle raising, with small farms, intensively cultivated, in the narrow valleys of the Pedernales and its smaller tributaries.[8]

Fredericksburg and New Braunfels became landmarks for other German immigrants in Texas seeking homes in the Hill Country. Within a short time other German-American communities were established at Boerne, Kendalia, Comfort, Center Point, Kerrville, Mason, Doss, Lukenbach, Albert, Hye, Stonewall, Twin Sisters, Cypress Mill, and scores of other locations in Gillespie, Mason, Comal, Blanco, Kendall, and Hays counties. As the German-American population of the Hill Country increased during the third and fourth quarters of the nineteenth century, the more recent arrivals tended to settle in the older communities already populated by a German element. These sturdy, self-sufficient people have made a fundamental contribution to the history of the state. As their historian, the late R. L. Biesele, has pointed out, the German settlers in Texas have "contributed particularly to the economic life of the state. They have been frugal and have been interested in home ownership. Some have been successful in various forms of business and industry. They have gone into all of the professions. They have generally participated in the political life of the state. . . . They have been interested in personal and religious freedom and have done their part to promote social organization and education."[9] Several years before the Civil War, at the time of the annual *Staats-Saengerfest,* delegates from

<hr>

[8] *Texas: A Guide to the Lone Star State* (New York, 1940), 636.
[9] *Handbook of Texas,* I, 684-685.

various local political clubs of the West Texas German communities met in San Antonio and adopted a resolution declaring that slavery was an evil and that the abolition of slavery should, be the business of the states, with the assistance, when needed of the federal government. Of course, the Anglo-American residents of Texas, having no understanding of the German attitude, looked on these people with great suspicion. When secession and war came, both were opposed by the German-Americans; and the Hill Country counties constituted an area of the Confederacy where Union sentiment ran strong. The result was that the German residents of the Hill Country counties of Kerr, Kendall, and Gillespie were persecuted by the Confederate government of Texas; the threats, martial law, and the Confederate pursuit of a band of Union sympathizers from the Guadalupe and Pedernales area and the subsequent battle of the Nueces represent another example of American intolerance toward the foreign-born in time of national emergency.[10]

While the activities of the Adelsverein were of prime importance in the advance of the frontier west of the Balcones fault, the buckskin-clad Anglo-Americans, veterans of generations of pioneering the American wilderness, were also attracted to the free and unoccupied lands beyond the Old San Antonio Road. Located at the slope of the Balcones, Hays County was pioneered by Thomas G. McGeehee, W. W. Moon, Mike Sessom, John D. Pitts, and others. The new county was created on March 1, 1848, and named for John Coffee Hays, the veteran ranger and Indian fighter. To the west of San Marcos and Stringtown, Wimberley was established in 1848 when William Winters built a saw and grist mill on the Blanco River. From the western part of Hays, the homesteaders soon followed the river or crossed Devil's Backbone to reach the unsurveyed lands along the mid-Blanco and Pedernales Rivers.

In the year 1836 Captain James Callahan camped in the Blanco River valley to hunt and fish; he was so impressed with the natural beauty of the land that in 1853 he returned with his family and some friends in search of a home. These pioneer stockmen built

---

[10]For information concerning Union sentiment in the counties of the Texas Hill Country and elsewhere in the state, see Claude Elliott, "Union Sentiment in Texas," *Southwestern Historical Quarterly*, L (April, 1947), 449.

cabins along the Blanco River near present Blanco, Texas, and prepared to defend themselves and their cattle from Indian attack. Through the efforts of the Pittsburgh Land Company, owned by Callahan and John D. Pitts, a town was surveyed and named Pittsburgh. When Blanco County was created and organized in the spring of 1858, the voters in the first election located the county seat across the river from Pittsburgh and named the new community Blanco City. Other settlements followed along the Blanco and Little Blanco rivers as other pioneer stockmen moved their herds into the hills and valleys of the new county. After a distinguished career as a journalist with the New Orleans *Picayune,* George Wilkins Kendall moved to Southwestern Blanco County (now Kendall County) in 1857 to establish a sheep ranch. During the early years, letters written by Kendall for publication in the New Orleans *Picayune* and the *Texas Almanac* influenced many settlers to come to the Blanco territory to try their hand at sheep ranching. John Speer, a Blanco pioneer, remembered that Kendall "influenced more men to come to Texas than almost any other man. Many inexperienced men engaged in the sheep business; a few succeeded; those who failed were called 'Kendall's victims.' "[11]

It was shortly after the organization of Blanco County in 1858 that the three sons of Jesse and Lucy Webb (Barnett) Johnson—Andrew Jackson, Jesse Thomas, and Sam Ealy Johnson, Sr.—pioneered the settlement of the Pedernales River valley to the north.

In the year 1846 Jesse and Lucy Webb (Barnett) Johnson moved their family from Georgia to Caldwell County, Texas, where they settled near Lockhart. Of the children that accompanied their parents to Texas, Andrew Jackson (Jack) Johnson had been born on January 27, 1835; Jesse Thomas (Tom) Johnson, July 6, 1836; and Samuel Ealy (Sam) Johnson, Sr., on November 12, 1838. After the deaths of Jesse and Lucy Johnson in 1857 and 1858, Andrew Jackson Johnson moved to Blanco County and settled on the north bank of the Pedernales River some four miles northeast of present Johnson City at the site of McCarty

[11]Bessie Brigham, "The History of Education in Blanco County" (unpublished M.A. thesis, University of Texas Library, Austin, Texas) ; Blanco County Scrapbook (Archives, University of Texas Library) ; John Speer, Blanco County History (unpublished Mss., Archives, University of Texas Library) , 12.

Spring; it was there that Jack Johnson built a double log cabin and entered the livestock business—raising sheep, horses, and cattle.[12]

In 1859 Samuel Ealy Johnson, Sr., accompanied his older brother, Jesse Thomas, for whom "he held great admiration and close attachment until Tom's death in 1877," to the Pedernales River valley. By the end of the year the two Johnson brothers were buying cattle in the vicinity of Fredericksburg and pasturing them on the open range in anticipation of a drive to the northern markets. Rebekah Baines Johnson records that in the late 1850's Sam and Tom Johnson "established their headquarters at [present] Johnson City," where they built a log cabin and a rock barn with portholes for use in case of Indian attack. Shortly after the outbreak of the Civil War, Sam E. Johnson, Sr., returned to Lockhart, where, on September 18, 1861, he enlisted in Company B, DeBray's Regiment, Confederate States Army. Tom Johnson later joined Captain R. J. Irving's Company of Blanco County, Third Frontier District, Texas State Troops. In the meantime Tom Johnson continued in the livestock business; and in the year 1864, as an agent for C. Herbert, Johnson rendered for taxes 320 acres of the James Provost land grant.[13] After the war Sam E. Johnson' returned to the Pedernales and joined his brother in a partnership cattle enterprise.

During the difficult years that followed the collapse of the Confederacy, many problems combined to challenge the moral fiber of the rugged individualists of the Hill Country and West Texas frontier. Those who lived through the two decades following the close of the war wrestled with the irritations of political reconstruction; the physical problem of drouth, flood, and frost; inadequate religious, educational, and medical facilities; the financial hardships brought on by low commodity prices and inadequate marketing facilities; and the ever-present danger of sudden death from Indian attack. Selected passages from the memoirs of John

---

[12]John Stribling Moursund, *Blanco County Families for One Hundred Years* (Austin, 1958), 208f; Scrapbook of Rebekah Johnson Bobbitt, compiled by Mrs. Rebekah Baines Johnson, in private collection of Rebekah Johnson Bobbitt, Austin, Texas.

[13]Moursund, *Blanco County Families,* 213. After extensive research in the Blanco County deed records, Moursund established the date of the establishment of the Johnson ranch as 1864-65.

Speer illustrate the difficulties of life along the Blanco County frontier:

I neglected to say that in the fall of 1865 the county officers were all turned out and a new set appointed, as follows James Odiorne Chief Justice M. F. Bell County Clerk J. W. Herrman Dist. Clerk Thos. F. Odiorne Sheriff Hiram Bryant commissioner. There was an election held in 1866 for county officers which resulted as follows Samuel Johnson Chief Justice. Thomas Morgan Dist. Clerk. Jno. W. Speer County Clerk. A. J. Kercheville Sheriff.

In this election politics were at a white heat and party split was at its highest. Much bad feeling was engendered, and of course great disappointment to the Salt River Party, and this was more potent for the defeated ones had been so sanguine of success that a grand barbecue was gotten up to celebrate the victory, as well as to do honor to Independence day, the 4th of July.

[1867]

In Feb. 1867 John P. Kellam rented out his place and moved to Stringtown. I think it was in this year that Joe Rogers moved to Hays County.

Some new settlers came in and began to open and improve farms, and establish stock ranches. The beef driving was carried on to some extent. A good many horses were driven off. Tom and Sam Johnson bought the Moss place near Johnson City and started a ranch. The planting of cotton increased, and was found to be profitable.

[1869]

Stock did well in the spring of 1869. Tom and Sam Johnson bought and drove out a large number of cattle. They bought mostly on credit, and during the summer and fall brought home some 10 or 12 two horse wagons and paid for the cattle they had driven out in the spring, and soon began to engage cattle and prepare for the next spring drive.

In the month of June, Tom Felps and his wife who lived on Cypress Creek were murdered by the Indians in sight of their home. Just after dinner they walked down to the creek (Cypress) to catch some fish; in a short time the Indians cut them off from the house and murdered them both near together. This made many sad hearts for they had many friends. They left two small children, a son and daughter.

On the 7th of July, 1869, was first overflow which did great damage to farms along the creeks and branches. The Blanco was higher than it had ever been known before. I was informed at this time that the stage from San Marcos to Austin was upset and swept away in the Blanco. Several persons were drowned . . . it was real good to stand off at a safe distance and see the Blanco on a grand tare. The largest harm done here by high water was the washing away of Harrison's mill at Blanco and Capt's mill above town. Some fences, wash pots, tubs, calves, setting hens, pigs, in fact everything that was loose that came within reach of the Blanco was washed away.[14]

During the late 1860's Tom and Sam Johnson's ranch on Williamson Creek and the Pedernales River became one of the best-known cattle operations in the Hill Country. On December 11, 1867, Sam E. Johnson, Sr., returned to Lockhart to marry Eliza Bunton, the daughter of Robert Desha and Jane (McIntosh) Bunton. The young couple returned to the Johnson ranch and began housekeeping in the log cabin that the Johnson brothers had built before the war. At this time Tom and Sam Johnson had title to the property adjacent to the confluence of Williamson Creek and the Pedernales River. Shortly after the Indian raid on Cypress Creek and the murder of Tom Felps and his wife, a small group of Blanco County rangers met a group of unidentified Indians in the Deer Creek fight. The Indians were routed, and the three rangers wounded in the fight—Alexander and George Roberts and Joe Bird—were carried to the Johnson ranch for medical aid. The extent of the Johnson boys' ranching operations was described by A. W. Capt, a veteran cowboy and trail driver; Capt recalled:

Beginning in the spring of 1870, when large herds were being driven from Texas up the Chisholm Trail to Kansas and beyond, I got my best experience joining the "roundup" for Sam and Thomas Johnson, then the largest individual trail drivers operating in Blanco, Gillespie, Llano, Burnet, Hays, Comal, and Kendall Counties, with headquarter pens and branding stall at the mouth of Williamson's Creek in Blanco County and headquarters at Johnson's ranch on the Pedernales River, Johnson City, the county site of Blanco County. The roundup or range hands and range boss usually gathered, road branded and delivered a herd of from 2,500 to 3,000 head of cattle, which a trail boss and his outfit received at headquarters ranch, but sometimes we delivered them at the Seven Live Oaks on the prairie west of Austin. After a good nights rest the ranch hands, bidding their relief "So long, we'll meet you later in Kansas," with pack and ponies hit the back trails for another herd for the next outfit.[15]

In the early winter of 1871 a young cowboy by the name of Horace M. Hall, a native of Charleston, Illinois, journeyed to

---

[14]John Speer, Blanco County History, 44f.
[15]J. Marvin Hunter, Trail Drivers of Texas (Bandera, 1924), 362-363.

Abilene, Kansas, in search of a job; he signed up with the Johnson ranch "outfit" and accompanied them on their return to Texas. In a series of letters to his father, Dr. Jesse Hall, the young cowhand revealed some interesting information about his employers. Writing from Abilene on November 1, 1871, Hall told the homefolks that "We are about to start to Texas with Sam Johnson, a big

Sam Ealy Johnson, Sr.

cattle dealer." A few days later Hall reported, "I am in Johnson's camp now, out at the cattle pens; and I am writing on the bread board in the smoke of the fire. . . . The boys have sold all of their cattle and tomorrow they will commence 'outfitting' and then go to Texas; hands here get from $30 to $100 a month and board. The Johnson boys have brought up 25 herds this season the smallest of which was 1500." After preparations for the return trip, the "Johnson boys" took their outfit home over the Texas Road or East Shawnee Trail. The Texas Road followed the Neosho River from near its headwaters to Baxter Springs, Kansas, then along the Grand River to a ferry crossing on the Arkansas River at Fort Gibson, Indian Territory. From Fort Gibson the trail led to a ferry crossing on the Red River near Sherman, Texas, and from the Red River southward across the Central Texas counties to the vicinity of Austin and home. On April 25, 1872, another letter written by young Hall from "johnsons Ranche, Blanco co Tex" reports that "We have been gathering cattle for the past month and now they have two herds about ready to start. . . . This is a beautiful country through here: mountains, clear rocky streams, live oaks, mesquite, with rich valleys & bottom lands for farming & mountains for stock, abondance of game & Indians once a year."[16]

The range-cattle industry during the 1870's and 1880's was a highly speculative venture. As the John Speer memoirs reveal, Sam and Tom Johnson bought their stock on credit, drove the herds to the Kansas railheads, and came home to pay their bills; evidently they had little left in the form of profit at the end of the year. Cattle prices were good in 1870, with the result that the drive from Texas in 1871 was the greatest in history, 700,000 head going to Kansas alone. Besides Texas cattle, the other western states were beginning to contribute to the beef supply and to reap the benefits of high prices. In 1871 the picture changed; there were few buyers—those were reluctant—and the bottom fell out of the market. For the effect of this changed situation on the fortunes of Jesse Thomas and Sam Ealy Johnson, the historian returns to the story told by the venerable John Speer:

The year 1871 set in cold, sleety, and disagreeable. Though with the fine crops of 1870 there was plenty. . . .

Tom Johnson, who with his brother Sam, had driven to Kansas in 1870, about 7,000 head of cattle, came home with one hundred thousand dollars; and at once began to pay up for cattle already driven, and to buy for this year's drive. They took receipts and very soon had a large carpet bag full, and in such a shape there is no

---

[16]Joseph S. Hall (ed.), "Horace M. Hall's Letters from Gillespie County, Texas, 1871-1873," *Southwestern Historical Quarterly*, LXII (January, 1959), 336f.

doubt in my mind that a good many beeves were paid for twice and some of them three times; and some of the cattle were never paid for as the Inspector's books were all there was to go by, and sometimes the cattle could not be identified by that, but when called on a third time to pay for the same steer I never heard of him [Tom Johnson] demanding a receipt ... but so it was that in a few months the Johnsons had paid out all of their money. ... Johnson had no trouble in getting cattle, and drove out this year about 10,000 head, and many trades were made and some notes taken, payable when Tom Johnson comes back from Kansas, but this was a hard year for the cattle drivers. The financial pressure was so great that the large drive of Texas cattle could not be sold and many, among them Johnson, were obliged to winter a large part of their cattle, and a great many died, Johnson lost heavily, and was forced to sacrifice some valuable property in Fredericksburg and a fine farm in Gillespie County. So with all his mishaps he failed to pay his debts, which was a great loss to the people, and destroyed confidence.[17]

Like hundreds of other Texas cattlemen during the so-called "golden age" of the range-cattle industry, Tom and Sam Johnson simply experienced a streak of bad luck; it is apparent, however, that their sad experience with an overstocked market and low prices was a severe setback to the young brothers. Tom Johnson, no doubt worn out by too many long days in the saddle in all kinds of weather, had only a few more years to live; his death came in the year 1877. Sam E. Johnson, Sr., moved his growing family to Caldwell County and later to the Northern Hays County town of Buda. Sometime during the winter of 1888-89 he returned to his beloved "mountains," to settle on a small farm in the Pedernales River valley between the villages of Stonewall and Hye. In recalling the late years of her father-in-law's life, Rebekah Baines Johnson remembered:

Highly gregarious, he attended all the neighborly meetings and met his friends with a handshake, friendly greetings, and a hearty resounding laugh. He seldom returned from these meetings without accompanying guests, and he was widely known for his hospitality and kind friendliness. A man of strong courage, deep convictions, and a calm philosophy which allowed no worry, he lived serenely and quietly at his pleasant country home on the bank of the Pedernales from 1888 until 1915, almost thirty years. Prior to that, he led a very active, energetic, often hazardous existence. He was a tall, lithe, well-built rangy man, six feet in height, with black wavy hair

---

[17]John Speer, Blanco County History, 59.

and blue eyes. His snowy beard and thick mane of white hair in his last years gave him a patriarchal appearance.

He loved to sit on the front porch of his farm home reading his Bible and his newspapers, and greeting the frequent visitors with a hearty invitation to get down and come right in for a visit. Although he had a high temper, he was seldom seen in anger and never in his life used an oath. He had a very deep and abiding faith in the Christadelphian creed.[18]

The end of life came for the aging Samuel Ealy Johnson on February 25, 1915, at his home near Stonewall; in his seventy-seven years he had left an imprint on the land in which he lived.

After the elder Sam Johnson moved to Caldwell and Hays counties for a temporary residence of a few years, Blanco County continued to grow and develop as new families moved into the region in search of homesteads. John Speer recalls that

The winter of 1874-75 was wet and very disagreeable, but stock wintered fairly well. . . . cotton continued to advance and by March 1875 was worth in New York 14 to 15¢, but for some cause there was a sudden collapse, and by midsummer it was down to 10 or 11¢.

Immigrants continued to come in, farms were enlarged and new ones opened. About this time it began to be said, "the range is broken played out" and we must depend on farming. But the close observer could see what this meant. It was to encourage the next neighbor to sell or move his stock out and make room for the shrewd old settler who was sure to keep all of his stock. But school experience, which sometimes exacts enormous tuition, has learned us all, including the thick skulls, who usually attend it, that farming alone is not the easiest or best way to make money, or even a living. But those who diversified their crops, raised a little stock, and took care of it; had a few beeves, horses or hogs; or a sack of wool to sell was the man that was in easy circumstances. . . . As we have intimated, the man that digs all of his living out of the ground has an uphill business of it, a "hard row to hoe." Our people continued to pay more attention to their orchards and gardens, and began to reap the reward.[19]

During the year 1879 the town of Johnson City was surveyed and established by James Polk (Jim) Johnson, the son of John Leonard Johnson and the nephew of Thomas Jesse and Sam E. Johnson, Sr. Coming to Texas from his native Alabama at an early

---

[18]Rebekah Johnson Bobbitt Scrapbook.
[19]John Speer, Blanco County History, 62.

age, James P. Johnson went to work for his uncles on the Johnson ranch after a period of military service in the Civil War. He helped them both on the home range and on the trail drives to Kansas. According to the Blanco County records, he acquired title to the Sam and Tom Johnson land in 1872-73. It was in the mid-1870's that James P. Johnson conceived the idea of founding a town and "getting the county seat moved from the town of Blanco to the new town." John S. Moursund points out in his *Blanco County Families* that

He had the cooperation of most of the residents in the northern part of the county. Efforts to call an election on the permanent location of the county seat in December of 1876 did not succeed. Then, in August of 1879, petitions of citizens from the northern part of the county were presented to the County Commissioners Court for an election on October 28th, 1879. Although the results of the election gave Blanco the victory by a small margin of seven votes, James P. Johnson went ahead with his plans for establishing a new town. Using a part of the James Fentress land grant [also a part of the old Johnson ranch property], ... prior to the election of 1879 he laid off the townsite, consisting of approximately 100 blocks, with one block being set aside for a public square and use of the site of the prospective court-house. Approximately 29 blocks were sub-divided into lots with each of the 29 blocks containing six lots. The new townsite was surveyed by John M. Watson, Surveyor of Blanco County, on September 29, 1879.[20]

It appears that the first lot in Johnson City was sold to W. W. Martin. During the early 1880's the small hamlet grew slowly; and, in 1891, Johnson City became the county seat of Blanco County. Located in the center of a ranching area, where cattle, Angora goats, and sheep have been raised down through the decades, Johnson City's agrarian nature has remained the keystone of the economic life of the community. During the 1890's a young boy by the name of Sam Ealy Johnson, Jr., was spending his early adolescent years on his father's farm to the west of Johnson City; in time he would become one of the leading citizens of the community and its political spokesman in state affairs. We now turn for a closer look at the life of a member of the second generation of Johnsons to be challenged by the stern nature of the Texas Hill Country.

---

[20] John S. Moursund, *Blanco County Families for One Hundred Years*, 210-211.

II.

SAM EALY JOHNSON, JR.: HILL COUNTRY DEMOCRAT

1

WHILE THE PRIMARY SOURCES ARE MEAGER, WIDELY SCATtered, and difficult to ferret out, the time has come to chronicle the life and political career of Sam Ealy Johnson, Jr., a grass-roots Democrat from the Texas Hill Country and the father of the thirty-sixth President of the United States.

The fifth child and first son of Sam Ealy and Eliza (Bunton) Johnson, Sam Ealy Johnson, Jr., was born on October 11, 1877, in the Northern Hays County community of Buda, Texas. Before the birth of his son the elder Sam Johnson took great pride in being the father of "the four prettiest girls in ten counties," but he resented the fact that his friends referred to him as "Gal Johnson." Needless to say, the birth of a son brought great joy to the Johnson household. Young Sam Johnson spent his childhood in the agrarian community of Buda and on his father's Pedernales River farm. With regard to these early years, it is remembered that

Eliza [Johnson], too, looked with great tenderness on this child whose dark eyes, black curls, and white skin were a Bunton inheritance and whose mental alertness and traits of leadership could be traced back to her beloved Deshas. So the precocious, attractive boy, Sam, was the darling of the home. Attired as nearly as possible like his father, he accompanied him whenever possible, and at an early age acquired an unusual poise and assurance. He had a quick mind, keen perception, and an amazing memory. . . . He was extremely active and loved all sports. When he was about eleven the Johnsons moved to Gillespie County locating on the Pedernales River near Stonewall. The tasks and delights of farm life presented a challenge to Sam; he must ride faster; plow longer, straighter rows; and pick more cotton than his companions. This sense of competition was a strong urge throughout his life.[1]

During the years of Sam Johnson, Jr.'s, youth, Blanco County remained a sparsely populated area with many frontier characteristics. In 1884, only three years before the Johnson family returned to the Pedernales, the Blanco *News* pointed out that the population of the county in 1880 was 3,583 inhabitants and that these people were, for the most part, "small farmers and stock-raisers." It was also pointed out that the largest farm in the county did not exceed 300 acres and "we are not ashamed that we have no big plantations, nor sheep or cattle kings."[2] As a part of this agrarian setting, Sam E. Johnson, Jr., longed for an education but found that his services on the farm were essential to the meager livelihood that resulted only from long hours of tilling the soil. Like many another youngster growing up in an agrarian community, young Sam could attend the local school at nearby Johnson City only at a great sacrifice on the part of his parents. At one time his father gave him a few cattle, saying, "Son, this is all that I can do for your schooling this year." After feeding the cattle for a few weeks, young Sam Johnson butchered his small herd of steers one by one, carved the meat into choice cuts, and peddled steaks, roasts, and soupbones throughout the communities of Stonewall and Hye. In this fashion he made enough money to carry him through the winter term at the Johnson City school. Later on, when the Johnson City barber took sick, Sam E. Johnson bought the unused barber chair and tools. After a few lessons (with the help of a few faithful friends who volunteered for free haircuts), young Sam became a full-fledged barber on Saturdays and during the late afternoons following a school day. His ability to devise money-making schemes ended when an attack of so-called "indigestion"

---

[1]Rebekah Baines Johnson in Rebekah Johnson Bobbitt's Scrapbook.
[2]Blanco County Scrapbook, Archives, University of Texas Library, Austin, Texas.

forced him to leave school for a rest on his Uncle Lucius Bunton's ranch near Marfa, Texas.[3]

No doubt Sam Johnson spent his days on the Bunton ranch dreaming of a college education which he knew to be impossible under the circumstances; by this time he wanted desperately to teach school. After a short visit in Marfa, young Johnson returned to the Pedernales farm. With the idea of becoming a schoolteacher primary in his mind, he purchased or borrowed thirteen books covering the academic subjects that comprised the standard examination for a teacher's certificate. With his books in hand, and armed with a bottle of pepsin pills and a sack of dried fruit (both recommended by his doctor), young Johnson sought the help of his Grandmother Bunton. Jane McIntosh Bunton—an educated woman and a skilled teacher—was glad to take her ambitious grandson into her home as a private pupil. Sam E. Johnson responded to his grandmother's teaching; and, after a few weeks of intensive preparation, he journeyed to Blanco and passed the examination leading to the coveted teacher's certificate. In later years he was proud of the fact that on the examination he scored 100 per cent on Texas and United States history—his two favorite subjects.[4]

In the fall of 1896 Sam Ealy Johnson, Jr., opened the winter term as the teacher at White Oak school near the small community of Sandy. White Oak was a typical one-room, rural Texas school where all sizes and all grades of students were taught in the same cramped quarters. To Sam Johnson, each student was an individual problem and challenge; as a result the young teacher varied his method of teaching to adjust to the needs of each of his many students. While a resident in the Sandy community, Johnson became a part of the household of a certain Mr. and Mrs. Young. The following winter, the school term of 1897-1898, young Johnson taught the Rocky school near Hye. Here he boarded with the Shipp family and loved to sit around the winter fire listening to Captain Rufus Perry tell of his experiences as an Indian fighter and ranger on the West Texas frontier.

Sam E. Johnson's teaching career ended with the close of the term at Rocky school in the late winter or early spring of 1898. By this time he wanted to study law; but finding it necessary to

---

[3]Rebekah Baines Johnson in Rebekah Johnson Bobbitt's Scrapbook.
[4]Ibid.

make a living, he rented his aging father's farm and moved into "the old house" that had been the first farm home of his parents. He and his hired hands operated the Johnson farm with success for several years around the turn of the century. Travelers along the river road often timed their journey "to make it to little Sam Johnson's by nightfall in order to spend the night and enjoy a good time." Among the many frequent visitors at the Johnson farm were W. C. Linden and Dayton Moses, both lawyers, and Kay Alexander, a teacher and engineer. During these years Sam Johnson's next-door neighbor, also basically a farmer, was his friend and brother-in-law, Clarence Martin.

It is quite probable that over the decades no person, with the exception of his immediate family, had a greater influence over the life of Sam E. Johnson, Jr., than Clarence W. Martin—farmer, lawyer, and judge. The son of Judge W. W. Martin, a pioneer resident of Blanco County, Clarence W. Martin was born at San Marcos, Texas, on November 26, 1879. After his marriage to Miss Frank Johnson, an older sister of Sam E. Johnson, Jr., Clarence Martin became a prominent resident of Blanco County and, in later years, of the Gillespie County community of Stonewall. After a study of law, Martin was drawn toward a career of public service— first as a justice of the peace in the town of Blanco, later as a member of the Texas House of Representatives from the old 98th District (Hays, Blanco, Gillespie, and Comal counties), and still later as District Judge of the 33rd Judicial District from 1902 until his resignation in 1915. In 1917 Martin became the chief defense attorney for Governor James E. Ferguson during the governor's impeachment trial. Martin practiced law in Austin and Fredericksburg until his death in August, 1936.[5]

After Martin's marriage to Frank Johnson, he became friend and counselor to young Sam E. Johnson. As the decades passed, the friendship of these two cross-fence neighbors deepened. It was Martin, to be sure, who interested Johnson in the possible study of law in the late 1890's; and it was Martin who first interested Johnson in local politics by urging him to be a candidate for the Texas Legislature in 1904. No doubt Martin was of great assistance to the young legislator in 1905 and in 1907. The Johnson-Martin

---

[5]Moursund, *Blanco County Families*, 280f.

association—based on mutual trust and respect—was to endure for the remaining years of the lives of these two men; democratic in philosophy and unselfish in service, they exemplify the finest qualities in the sterling character of Texas Hill Country folk.

In 1904 Sam E. Johnson, Jr., was elected to the state legislature from the 89th Representative District. Rebekah Baines Johnson remembered that at the time of his election he was "a personable young man, slender and graceful, immaculately groomed, agreeable and affable in manner and with great personal magnetism. He was happy and interested in his work. He felt keenly and understood with clarity the needs of his state, and worked conscientiously and effectively on beneficial and needed legislation."[6]

When young Sam Ealy Johnson arrived in Austin in January, 1905, to claim his chair in the House of Representatives of the 29th Legislature, the political cross-currents in Texas reflected a tug-o-war between the agrarian liberals of the previous decade on one hand and the ever-present conservative philosophy of the business and financial interests on the other. The governor of the state was S. W. T. Lanham, a conservative underling of Edward M. House, the well-to-do planter who "made politics an avocation and soon surpassed those who made it a profession."[7] While it may be said that the general tone of Texas politics was conservative at this time, it is interesting to note that the voices of discontent—so adequately expressed during the golden age of Populism and the Hogg administrations—were not altogether silenced. As the election of 1906 approached, public sentiment swung definitely away from conservatism as Thomas M. Campbell took up the Hogg protests of an earlier era. Running on a platform featuring a call for war on the trusts, an anti-lobby law, and tax reform, Campbell won the nomination after a hard fight and carried the November election without difficulty. It was at this time that the issues of tax reform, prohibition, and J. W. Bailey's relations with oil companies rose to produce strife within the ranks of the Democratic Party.

From the first day of the regular session of the House of Representatives, Sam Ealy Johnson, Jr., exhibited a brand of agrarian

---

[6]Rebekah Baines Johnson in Rebekah Johnson Bobbitt's Scrapbook.

[7]Rupert N. Richardson, *Texas: the Lone Star State* (Englewood Cliffs, 1958), 365.

liberalism that was to be the primary characteristic of his long and distinguished career of public service. Assigned to the committees on public lands and judicial districts, Johnson joined six others (including Ferg Kyle of Hays County and W. W. Burnett of Kerr County), to introduce a bill authorizing the governor "to purchase the land which was a part of the Alamo mission in San Antonio" and setting aside an appropriation of $65,000 for that purpose. In addition to the Alamo Purchase Act, Johnson introduced a bill prohibiting calf-roping contests—he had always considered roping contests as a cruel and inhumane sport—and a motion, true to his agrarian electorate, to exempt Blanco County from the provisions of a previous wolf-scalp law which required county commissioners to pay a small fee for each wolf scalp brought in from the field and pasture. In the days that followed, Johnson gave his support to and served on the Free Conference Committee that ironed out the differences between the House and Senate versions of the famous Terrell Election Law of 1905; he also supported bills to tax insurance, telephone, and sleeping and dining car companies; to regulate, through city councils, rates charged by public utility companies (water, gas, and electric power) in certain towns and cities; to prevent fraud and deception in the manufacture of articles of food and drink (a pure-food bill); to levy a franchise tax on corporations doing business within the state, and to establish a juvenile court system for Texas. Altogether, it may be said that Sam Ealy Johnson represented his constituents with distinction as a first-year man in the 29th Legislature.[8]

In the summer of 1906 Johnson decided to buck tradition and stand for re-election. Strange as it may seem to present-day political observers, it was then the well-established custom in the 89th Representative District (Blanco, Gillespie, Kendall, and Llano counties) that the position of representative would be rotated among the member counties at each successive election. The result was, of course, that a one-term legislator had no chance at all to establish himself and become a part of the inner workings of the state capital. In the spring of 1906 W. A. Wright, editor of the Blanco *News,* who fully realized the weakness of the custom, expressed his opinion:

[8]*House Journal, Regular Session, 29th Legislature,* pp. 56-1494 (hereafter cited as H. J.).

One term merely introduces a man, you might say to the legislative body. He can do better work in succeeding terms than the first. Hon. Sam E. Johnson of Gillespie County has been there but one term. He has served to good purpose, but could still do better service in succeeding terms and could have his legislative career rounded out better were he to remain a second term. We thought from a recent talk with him that it was his intention to seek to fill the office a second term and then yield to Llano County. Should Llano County send a man to Austin this year, he would have to get down and out next term for Blanco, and so it goes. We don't like such quick and successive changes, unless we have a "bad man" in office. ... We hope it will be the future policy of the party to keep their man in this position more than one term.[9]

A few weeks later Wright published in his Blanco newspaper an article from the San Antonio *Express* to the effect that

Representative S. E. Johnson of Fredericksburg is one of the hard working members of the House. Although he is serving his first term in the Legislature he has made a splendid reputation for himself and should he return for a second term he would be in a position to render still more useful service to his constituents. It has been the custom in the past in Mr. Johnson's district to give each county a turn about in sending representatives to the Legislature, but this practice will probably be broken in Mr. Johnson's case as his service is considered of such value as to entitle him to a second term. ... Mr. Johnson has made a good representative and if Llano is satisfied to let him return another term Blanco and Gillespie would be more than satisfied.[10]

In spite of the fact that there was considerable Johnson sentiment in Llano County, David Martin of Llano, proprietor of the Martin Telephone Company, announced his candidacy for representative on April 19, 1906, "under the rotation rule that has been observed in this district for some time."[11] On the last day of May the Blanco *News* carried an announcement of Johnson's decision to run, with the following explanation:

Hon. S. E. Johnson, Jr., of Gillespie County, announces as a candidate for re-election to the Legislature from this district. Mr. Johnson had no intention of making the race at first, recognizing that under the rule adopted in this district, heretofore, it was Llano County's

---

[9]Blanco *News*, March 1, 1906.

[10]*Ibid.*, March 29, 1906.

[11]*Ibid.*, April 19, 1906.

time to present the candidate. But Llano County, while she has a candidate, has solicited Mr. Johnson so urgently to run again that he has finally decided to do so. ... Mr. Johnson has made a fine record in the last legislature and for that reason Llano is desirous of having him represent the district again; at least quite a number of them wish it.[12]

A spirited contest resulted. Typical of the political rallies of the era was the two-day Fourth-of-July celebration held on the banks of the Blanco River at Blanco. Besides music by the New Braunfels Brass Band, the events of the two days included a baseball game between the Johnson City and Blanco teams, foot races, hurdle races, sack races, and political speeches by Judge W. W. Burnett, Judge S. W. Wallace, Sheriff J. R. Johnson, Claude Gray, J. C. Goar, Thad Cage, Oscar Branch Colquitt, David Martin, and Sam Ealy Johnson, Jr.[13] In addition to events such as the ones named above, the campaign trail included a series of elm and live-oak grove picnics (featuring political speeches, band concerts, and baseball) , church and community ice-cream suppers, and the more arduous task of house-to-house and farm-to-farm electioneering along the back roads of the region. On the eve of the party primary, the Llano *Times* endorsed Johnson over Martin, and the venerable W. A. Wright of the Blanco *News* pleaded: "Llano, don't claim it now. It is better to give a man two terms than to have a new man every two years. Boys, get out and shell the woods, and let the people choose this day whom they will send to Austin to help make their laws." On the day of the primary (July 26) Johnson carried Blanco County by a vote of 314 to 48 and won a decisive victory over Martin.[14]

When Sam Ealy Johnson returned to Austin in January, 1907, for the regular session of the 30th Legislature, he was placed on the committee on agriculture and on the committee on public printing; later in the session he was appointed to the committee on public lands and to the committee on roads, bridges, and ferries.[15] This latter appointment is of great significance since it marks the beginning of three decades of service in the quest of

---

[12]*Ibid.*, May 31, 1906.
[13]*Ibid.*, June 14, 1906.
[14]*Ibid.*, July 26, 1906; August 9, 1906.
[15]H. J., Regular Session, 30th Legislature, 156f, 210, 216.

good roads for Texas; Johnson was one of the pioneers in the present Texas Good Roads Association. In the early days of the session Johnson had a chance to express himself on a most controversial matter—the choice of a United States Senator.

In 1901 Joseph Weldon Bailey, after a period of distinguished service in the Congress of the United States from the old Fifth District, was elected to the United States Senate by the legislature to succeed Senator Horace Chilton. During Bailey's first term in the Senate, he was accused of accepting a $100,000 fee as legal counsel for the Waters-Pearce Oil Company and of similar conflict-of-interest association with the Standard Oil Company and with the John H. Kirby lumber interest of East Texas. These accusations, whether true or false, provided much fuel for the political fires in 1906-1907, and Bailey became a controversial figure in the Democratic Party of Texas. Though Senator Bailey was re-elected in January, 1907, pending an investigation by the legislature, seven members of the House of Representatives refused to cast their votes for him; and Sam E. Johnson was one of the seven. In explaining his vote, Johnson reasoned:

In reciting my reasons for not voting for or against Hon. Joseph Weldon Bailey, for re-election to the United States Senate, I do so, believing it to be for the best interest of the people of Texas. . . . and believing that the private and official acts of Senator Bailey warrant the House of Representatives in demanding a full, fair, and impartial investigation of the charges made against Senator Bailey. . . . If this committee finds Senator Bailey innocent of the charges filed against him, then it would give me pleasure to vote for him. It is a well known fact that I have been for a full investigation of his conduct, and it would not be consistent for me to vote for him at this time.[16]

In the three months that followed, Johnson introduced a bill to provide for the transportation of children to school districts in adjacent counties and a bill designed to protect stock raisers and farmers by providing for the destruction of wolves and other wild animals with a state "reward" as the motivating factor. It is worthy of note that he continued his agrarian liberalism by supporting legislative measures to regulate lobbying, to tax express companies carrying intoxicating liquors in dry territories, to cre-

[16]*Ibid.*, 204.

ate the office of county superintendent of schools, and to establish the eight-hour day for railroad telegraphers. During the course of the legislative session, he also presented and endorsed a petition from the Farmers' Union of Lone Grove, Llano County, asking that, in legislating against gambling on cotton futures, care be exercised so as not to deprive "the merchants of the country of the medium of transacting a legitimate cotton business."[17] During the regular session of the 30th Legislature, W. J. Joyce, the chaplain, described "S. E. Johnson, Jr., of Hye," as follows: "Like many others, he is a quiet worker. His pleasant, gentlemanly ways secure to him the friendship of all the members. Will bear gentle reproof, but will kick like a mule at any attempted domination."[18]

On August 20, 1907, after a "whirlwind courtship," Sam Ealy Johnson, Jr., married Rebekah Baines, the daughter of Joseph W. and Ruth (Huffman) Baines. The son of Reverend George W. Baines, a Baptist minister and educator, Joseph W. Baines moved from Louisiana to Texas with his family in 1850 to settle in the rural community of Anderson in Grimes County. After attending Baylor University and serving in the Confederate Army, 1863-1865, J. W. Baines began teaching school in Collin County, where, in 1869, he married Ruth Huffman. He studied law under ex-Governor J. W. Throckmorton and edited the McKinney *Advocate*. A staunch Democrat, Baines gave John Ireland such energetic support in his race for governor in 1882 that Ireland appointed him Secretary of State. As a result the Baines family moved to Austin in 1883, and J. W. Baines proved to be a valuable assistant to the John Ireland administration. With regard to the significant traits of Joseph W. Baines, it is recorded that

High-minded, generous, and kind, he was a devoted husband and father, an altruistic, industrious civic and church leader, a friend to the poor and needy. He loved the good and the beautiful, was a devout Christian, an untiring worker in every field that engaged his interest. When urged to join various societies or orders, he would always reply, "I am a Baptist and a Democrat, that is enough for me."[19]

[17]*Ibid.*, 76, 66of, 754ff.

[18]*Ibid.*, 427.

[19]John S. Moursund, *Blanco County Families*, 11-12.

Joseph W. Baines

At the close of the Ireland term of office, J. W. Baines moved his family to Blanco, Texas; it was here that Rebekah Baines spent her girlhood in a lovely two-story limestone home overlooking the sparkling waters of the Blanco River. Rebekah Baines was born at McKinney, Texas, on June 26, 1881. In remembering her childhood and youth, she has written:

I was fortunate in being the first-born of my parents, a happy circumstance of superior advantage. My choice of parents was most felicitous; they were a happy, well-adjusted, and devoted couple who welcomed me into a well-ordered, peaceful home to which cross words and angry looks were foreign.

At an incredibly early age, my father taught me to read; reading has been one of the great pleasures and sustaining forces of my life. He taught me how to study, to think and to endure, the principles of mathematics, the beauty of simple things. He taught me that "a lie is an abomination of the Lord" and to all people the world over; he taught me obedience and self-control, saying that without them no one is worthy of responsibility or trust. He gave the timid child self confidence. My mother was the cheeriest, most energetic, and serenest of persons. . . She had great sanity, sweetness, and purity.

I am grateful for the little town of Blanco, my excellent teachers, men of ability and education not often found in such small places, my Baptist upbringing, sermons, prayer meetings, Sunday school; the splendid young people who were my companions and classmates—the Alexanders, Bells, Capts, Edwardses, Brighams, and Stubbses, many of them have gone far in the world; and all the neighborliness, the delights, the chores, and the charms of that simple, friendly, dearly loved town, Blanco. I love to think of our home, a two-story rock house with a fruitful orchard of perfectly spaced trees, terraced flower beds, broad walks, purple plumed wisteria climbing to the roof, fragrant honeysuckle at the dining room windows whose broad sills were seats for us children. Most of all I love to think of the hospitality of that home, of the love and trust, the fear of God, and the beautiful ideals that made it a true home.[20]

Following a severe financial reverse in 1903, J. W. Baines moved his family to Fredericksburg in 1904; it was there, after a lingering illness, that he died on November 18, 1906. It was shortly after her father's death that young Sam E. Johnson came into Rebekah Baines's life. Remembering these tender but difficult years, Rebekah recalled:

In 1903 my father suffered severe and sudden financial reverses. I am glad to say that we adjusted cheerfully to the financial change. My brother sold his rubber-tired buggy and returned to A and M College where he worked to defray his expenses until he received his degree. I took charge of the college book store at Baylor College to pay my expenses for my final year there. My father, however, grieved over his inability to continue his generous provision for his family, and his health became greatly impaired. He sought a new location

---

[20]Rebekah Baines Johnson in Rebekah Johnson Bobbitt's Scrapbook.

for his legal practice and moved to Fredericksburg in 1904. After a lingering illness, he passed away on November 18, 1906; so was broken our family circle. This was the first sorrow of my life, and it required all my determination and strength of will to adjust myself to life without my father, who had been the dominant force in my life as well as my adored parent, revered mentor, and most interesting companion.

We moved into the little home which my father had designed and had built and which had engaged his last loving thoughts of provision for his family. I continued teaching Expression classes and corresponding for daily newspapers. Fredericksburg might have been transplanted from the old world, its customs, ideas, and pursuits were unique and foreign; the people were thrifty, hard-working, honest, and self-respecting; most of all they were kind and their friendliness warmed our lonely saddened years. Mrs. Oscar Krauskopf and Mr. Alfred Vander Stucken will be remembered with gratitude all of my days. I presented plays with the help of the music teacher, Miss Ophelia Brown. I had a small congenial circle of friends: Julia Estill, Elizabeth and Frank Hanisch, Lorlie Wahrmund, Charlie Darrough, Emil Sauer, Alfred Brodie, and Dr. Peden, and his sister, Ada. The quiet unexciting associations of this period were enlivened by frequent visits from a dashing and dynamic young legislator, Sam Johnson. He took me to the Confederate Reunion where we enjoyed the oratory of senators Joe Bailey and Charlie Culberson, and Governor Tom Campbell. With his sister, Lucie, and brother, George, we heard William Jennings Bryan, whom we both admired extravagantly, address the legislature. He was enchanted to find a girl who really liked politics. We were married August 20, 1907, and moved out to the farm on the Pedernales River in Gillespie County. . . . And so began a new life for me.[21]

4

We will return to Rebekah Johnson's "new life" in the chapter that follows. To continue with Sam E. Johnson's political career, he did not stand for re-election in 1908 and was succeeded by William Bierschwale of Fredericksburg. It is noteworthy, however, that the old one-term tradition ceased to prevail in the 89th Representative District, a change for the better that must be attributed to Sam E. Johnson. Though not a candidate for public office during the decade between 1908 and 1918, Johnson was never far removed from the Texas political scene. Locally, he became a part of "the establishment" that made the political decisions and ruled the scene in Blanco and Gillespie counties; other members of the

---

[21]*Ibid.*

group included N. T. Stubbs, A. J. Wagner, A. W. Moursund, Sr., Clarence W. Martin, Ben Jack Stubbs, and others. On the national level, like so many other Texans, Johnson was a warm admirer of the progressive legislation that comprised Woodrow Wilson's "New Freedom." On the state level he gave his energetic support to the political career of James E. (Farmer Jim) Ferguson, one of the two liberal governors of the last half century of Texas politics.

Despite his benighted attitude toward the University of Texas and the cause of academic freedom, Texas historians and political scientists point out that the administrations of the Fergusons—James E. and Miriam—rank with those of Thomas Campbell and James E. Allred as the most liberally oriented of the present century. Writing of the Fergusons, Fred Gantt, Jr., calls attention to the fact that "the two governors were people of liberal minds. This is evident through official acts and public utterances over a long period of years. Mr. Ferguson's last political speeches were made for the re-election of President Roosevelt for a third term."[22] In commenting on "liberal democrats before 1962," three political scientists have recently pointed out that "whatever their personal faults, the Fergusons constantly preached for the poor farmer, opposed prohibition, and attacked the Ku Klux Klan." In retrospect it seems that for these stands alone they well deserve the liberal label.[23]

Although most Texas governors since 1900 have definitely been inclined toward the right of center, James E. Ferguson, a man whose influence in Texas politics spanned a generation, appeared on the scene in 1914 as the champion of the tenant farmer. At that time farm tenancy had been increasing each passing year, and the outlook of the tenant farmer, the more recent representative of the "poor whites" of the Old South, was discouraging indeed. In his campaign against Thomas H. Ball, of Houston, Ferguson proposed a law fixing farm rentals at one third of the cotton and one fourth of the other crops—a plank of the Ferguson platform that appealed to the agrarian renters of the state and to liberal thinkers everywhere. From the Panhandle to the Rio Grande and from the Piney

---

[22]Fred Gantt, Jr., *The Chief Executive in Texas: A Study in Gubernatorial Leadership* (Austin, 1964), 324.

[23]James R. Soukup, Clifton McCleskey, and Harry Holloway, *Party and Factional Division in Texas* (Austin, 1964), 91.

Woods to El Paso, tens of thousands of Texans—representatives of that broad generalization known as "the common man"—rallied to the banner of Jim Ferguson. It can be said without fear of exaggeration that Texas today is well-populated by a generation descended from a considerable number of sturdy folk who would have fought in the back alley for James E. and Miriam Ferguson; of course, a substantial number have become so well-heeled financially since the first World War that they can now afford to vote Republican and even espouse the philosophy of the extreme right-wing element of the region.

Among the early adherents to the Ferguson cause were Sam E. Johnson, Jr., and Clarence Martin of Gillespie County. Following the old Texas adage "If God's willing and the creeks don't rise," Martin and Johnson stumped every hollow, plateau, and village in Gillespie, Llano, Blanco, and Kendall counties in support of the Ferguson ticket. Recalling her Uncle Sam Johnson's efforts in behalf of Ferguson, Ava Johnson Cox recalls that "as time went on, he was a great supporter of Jim Ferguson; he campaigned wholeheartedly for him." Others recall that at the country dances of 1914 and 1916, Judge Clarence Martin composed the following square dance call:

Up Peeler and down McCall,
Swing your corners and promenade the hall.
Up Peeler and down McCall,
Vote for Jim Ferguson and scratch old Ball.[24]

When the votes came in from the forks of the creek and from the urban areas of the state, the results showed that Ferguson had defeated Ball handily by a vote of 237,062 to 191,558; in Gillespie County the vote was 1,215 to 95 in favor of Ferguson. Johnson and Martin had been effective in their campaign. The margin of victory for Ferguson was even greater in the November election. In the years that followed, Sam E. Johnson continued his unselfish support of Ferguson. Successful in the election of 1916—again he carried the Hill Country counties—Ferguson soon had difficulties with the Board of Regents, the president, and the faculty of the University of Texas. This trouble, coupled with a fearsome reaction that followed in the wake of the farm-tenant law, led to his

---

[24]Ava Johnson Cox to W. C. P., August 14, 1964.

impeachment and removal from office in September, 1917. During the dark days of the impeachment proceedings, Clarence W. Martin served as Ferguson's chief counsel for the defense; an interested spectator was Sam E. Johnson, Jr. It is not beyond the realm of probability that Ferguson's removal motivated Johnson, in part, to re-enter politics in 1918.

Sam E. Johnson, Jr., began his second and most fruitful period of service in the Texas legislature early in the year 1918. When the United States entered the war against Germany and the Central Powers in April, 1917, the 87th Representative District (renumbered but still including the same counties) was represented in Austin by Tom J. Martin, a resident of Fredericksburg. An officer in the Texas National Guard, Martin reported for duty at Camp Bowie, Texas, in the fall of 1917 and on January 18, 1918, resigned his post in the legislature.[25] As a result, Governor W. P. Hobby called a special election for Blanco, Gillespie, Llano, and Kendall counties to be held on February 15, 1918, to choose Martin's successor. A week before the election Robert Penniger of the Fredericksburg *Standard* reported that "S. E. Johnson of Blanco County is the only candidate that has announced, and will no doubt be elected. However, at this critical time it is highly important that everyone go to the polls and cast a vote. A special session of the legislature is soon to be called."[26]

Victorious in the special election, Sam Ealy Johnson attended the momentous special session of the 35th Legislature called by Governor Hobby to consider the so-called wartime amendments to the United States Constitution and other pressing matters. Undoubtedly the most regrettable feature of the "home front" during these months was the ugly intolerance bred by the war. Texas was no different in this regard from the rest of the nation, and by the spring of 1918 a militant anti-German sentiment was in full swing throughout the Lone Star State. The German-Americans of the Hill Country felt the pressure of a hostile public opinion soon after America's entry into the conflict. By the fall of 1917 Loyalty Leagues had been organized in many communities, including Fredericksburg, as a part of an effort by Texans of German descent

---

[25]Fredericksburg *Standard,* November 24, 1917; January 18, 1918.
[26]*Ibid.,* February 9, 1918.

to prove their loyalty to the United States. These efforts were to no avail, however, as the hate-Germany hysteria mounted with each passing week. In the spring of 1918 the special session of the 35th Legislature enacted a drastic law designed to promote loyalty in Texas. This law, known as House Bill 15, specified that any person, at any time or place, using disloyal or abusive language in the presence or hearing of another person, concerning the entry of the United States of America into or continuation of the war or concerning the army, navy, marine corps, flag, standard, color, or the uniform would be guilty of a felony and subject to imprisonment ranging from two to twenty-five years. It was this provincial attempt to legislate loyalty into being that aroused Sam E. Johnson to make one of his best-known speeches on the floor of the House of Representatives. Seeing no need for such a drastic measure, Johnson pleaded for a form of tolerance where patriotism would be tempered with common sense and justice. When he found himself in a minority, Johnson continued his fight against the bill and succeeded in defeating the section that would have granted the power of arrest to every Texas citizen.[27]

When the special session came to an end after weeks of bitter wrangling, Johnson visited Fredericksburg and "related his experiences as a member of the so-called War Legislature" to the the editor of the *Standard;* Robert Penniger reported to his readers that

Although sentiment ran high during this session, even in legislative halls, Johnson stood by his promises and voted against prohibition and kindred measures. He knew from the start that the small bunch of liberals would lose out in the maelstrom of fanatical propaganda, but he stood by his promise and voted accordingly, notwithstanding unfounded and vicious attacks on his character as a loyal American citizen.

Everybody knew beforehand that this session of the Legislature would be turbulent, and would show an overwhelming majority for prohibition. The acceptance of the office by Mr. Johnson was really a great sacrifice, and the voters should acknowledge their approval of the course Mr. Johnson followed, and thank him for the unselfish representation of our people.

Through his personal influence with Senators he succeeded in eliminating the paragraph of the Loyalty Bill which bestowed the

[27]Fredericksburg *Standard,* March 23, 1918; April 6, 1918; Rebekah Baines Johnson in Rebekah Johnson Bobbitt's Scrapbook.

Sam Ealy Johnson, Jr.

power of arrest upon every citizen and was a most dangerous provision for the peaceful civil status of citizenship as a whole.

Concluding by pointing out that "Mr. Johnson voted for the Suffrage Bill for women" in the referendum but opposed its ratification in the legislature, Penniger voiced his opinion that "he has served his people faithfully, and his just claims for higher honors at the hands of the voters, whenever made, will be willingly granted."[28]

[28]*Ibid.*, April 6, 1918.

In the summer of 1918 Johnson was renominated by the voters in the Democratic Party primary without opposition; but in the November election he was opposed by his Stonewall neighbor, August M. Benner, a Republican who ran as an "independent." A spirited contest resulted in which Johnson was the victor, but after which Benner filed a contested election plea which alleged that his name had been omitted from the official ballot in Kendall County and that "undue influence and intimidation had been practiced in Blanco County to influence voters" in favor of Johnson. When the 36th Legislature assembled at Austin in January, 1919, the Committee on Privileges, Suffrage, and Elections quickly determined the contest in favor of Johnson, pointing out that there were no facts to substantiate Benner's charges.[29]

In the regular session of the 36th Legislature, which began on January 14, 1919, Sam E. Johnson served on the revenue and taxation committee and on the agriculture committee. As the weeks of the two-month session passed, Johnson supported a bill to define livestock commission merchants; a bill reorganizing the Texas Ranger force; a bill (which he introduced) to regulate the pay of road hands, teams, and overseers in Gillespie County; a bill regulating the employment of women and minors and establishing an Industrial Welfare Commission to deal with such employment "and fix a minimum wage"; a bill providing free textbooks for public school children; and a bill appropriating state money to aid drouth-stricken farmers in obtaining seed and feed—the seed "to be planted by those who are too poor and unable to obtain seed," and the feed to be used "for the workstock of such people." In addition, Johnson worked for the passage of a resolution favoring Woodrow Wilson's Fourteen Points, a resolution favoring the League of Nations, a resolution requesting the Texas Congressional delegation to take steps "to obtain legislation stabilizing the value of cotton" so that a "reasonable profit" could be guaranteed to cotton producers; a resolution requesting President Wilson to return the railroads to private owners; and a resolution opposing continued government ownership of telephone and telegraph lines.

A week after adjournment of the regular session, the Blanco County *Record,* the Johnson City weekly newspaper, noted that

---

[29]H. J., 36th Legislature, 166-167.

Hon. S. E. Johnson and little son Lyndon were among the prominent visitors in Johnson City on Wednesday of this week. Mr. Johnson has one of the largest and best farms in this section of Texas, and has been kept quite busy of late supervising its cultivation. He has been too busy to devote much time to politics, but is keeping posted through the daily press. While we do not speak with authority, it is our opinion that Mr. Johnson will be a candidate to succeed himself as Representative of the 87th district. He has made such a splendid record that the district cannot afford to overlook his usefulness for another term. While Mr. Johnson has done a great deal for his home county, he has not overlooked the interests of other counties in the district and in casting his vote upon all important questions, has in such matters followed the expressed wishes of his constituents. The 87th district needs a man of Mr. Johnson's caliber in the next legislature and the Record knows of no other man in the district who could so ably fill this place.[30]

In the fall of 1920 Sam Ealy Johnson announced for re-election. The Blanco County *Record* pointed out:

Responding to the demands of petitions circulated in the four counties, Blanco, Llano, Kendall, and Gillespie, Hon. S. E. Johnson announces in this issue of the Record as a candidate of the 87th District.

Mr. Johnson's long and active career in the Legislature commends his services for reelection for he has during these eight years of service acquired a wide acquaintance with state officials, a far reaching influence among his colleagues, and a thorough knowledge of the procedures necessary for the enactment of prompt and efficient laws. As the daily papers of the State term it, "Johnson is a 'go-getter' and always succeeds in passing any legislation he introduces." In proof of his prompt action is his recent passage of the amendment to the tick-eradication law during the last two weeks call session. Having been selected by the Cattle Raisers Association to introduce the bill, he was complimented by the Governor and Attorney General's Department on his quick work.

The farmers of West Texas will recall with gratification the aid Johnson rendered in his passage of the bill appropriating over $2,000,-000 for the drouth stricken to obtain seed and feed to produce crops during the dry years. Many of the congratulatory telegrams from various Chambers of Commerce throughout West Texas on the passage of this bill urged Mr. Johnson to enter the race for Congress.

The State Department of Education recently promised Mr. Johnson aid for the rural schools of this district, enabling all to have seven months free school.

---

[30]Blanco County *Record*, March 26, 1920.

We feel that with the pressing need for good roads, more Federal and State aid for the same, longer and better term schools, and real representation of our people and their interests, we cannot at this time dispense with the services of this live and efficient officer. The legislation he has put through has promptness, (having passed three local bills in the 3rd call session and two in the last), his strenuous labor for good roads, and his unfailing devotion to his people, influence us to feel confident that the people of Blanco County will at the polls give him the large and well merited majority he has always received from the people who know him best.[31]

On the following day the Fredericksburg *Standard* joined the Johnson bandwagon by calling attention to the following facts: (1) Johnson voted against the national prohibition amendment; (2) he voted against the universal suffrage amendment; (3) at a time "when the Legislature wanted to prohibit the teaching of German at the State University, Mr. Johnson voted against the bill"; and (4) "at a time when the propaganda of hate against Americans of German descent was most violent, Mr. Johnson gave lie to slanders that were circulated in the legislature about the good citizens of German blood of this district." The *Standard* concluded with the remark that S. E. Johnson was endorsed by ex-Senator Julius Real, ex-Representative William Bierschwale, and ex-Representative W. A. Trenckman of Austin. It was also pointed out that Johnson had recently been appointed by the governor to attend the National Good Roads Convention, and that Johnson, the "independent candidate for the legislature is a farmer by profession and knows the needs of the farmer."[32]

Johnson was opposed by H. R. Smith, Felix J. Walch, and A. M. Benner. As early as the first week of August, T. R. Glidden, of the Blanco County *Record,* visited Fredericksburg "to confer with the businessmen and others about the political situation"; returning home, he wrote:

We were informed that Gillespie County was not responsible for the bringing out of A. M. Benner for Representative of the 87th District, and a great majority of the people do not favor his candidacy. In fact we do not know, or believe, that anyone in particular solicited Mr. Benner to run. But we do know that the district cannot afford to carry the joke too far, at this time.[33]

[31]*Ibid.,* October 15, 1920, p. 1.
[32]Fredericksburg *Standard,* October 16, 1920.
[33]Blanco County *Record,* Johnson City, August 6, 1920.

A week before the election Glidden defended Sam Johnson's vote against the 19th amendment as follows:

As a last resort a few of the opponents of Hon. S. E. Johnson have been busily engaged turning over the political stones with the vague hope that "something" would be found that would help the "lost cause." The "political monster" has been unearthed and here it is in all hideousness. . . . Hist! On the dead quiet now, sound the tocsin gently. It has been diskivered that the said Samuel E. Johnson, did once upon a time, with malice and forethought, knowingly and willfully cast his vote in favor of submitting an amendment to the voters of Texas to determine whether or not the good women of this state should have the right to vote. Now wouldn't this political offense jar your mother's preserves!

Setting the facts straight, the editor reported that S. E. Johnson had voted to submit the amendment to the people in a referendum election and that he voted for woman's suffrage "in the primary election" but opposed ratification in the legislature because his constituents in the district opposed it in the referendum; Glidden therefore reasoned that "his [Johnson's] political enemies evidently do not care for women votes" and "the good women" of the 87th District "should bear this in mind" on election day.[34]

After all of the shouting and the tumult, the *Record* gleefully reported that "Sam E. Johnson was elected over all three of his opponents by a majority of between 1000 and 1500 votes." There appeared to be no doubt in the mind of one country editor that the best man won.[35]

Re-elected in 1922, Johnson rendered what was probably his greatest public service as a member of the 37th and 38th Texas legislatures in 1921 and 1923 respectively. In the 37th Legislature he introduced a measure providing for a new road law for Llano County, another bill providing for free passes on railroads for persons receiving state pensions, a bill directing the legislature to provide for the construction and operation of a system of public highways, and a bill providing for the appointment of a state forester. Two years later, in the regular session of 1923, Johnson introduced a bill "to protect wild birds and wild fowl in the Edwards Plateau region of Texas" and voted for a corporation tax, an occupation tax on sulphur production, and an occupation tax

[34]*Ibid.*, October 29, 1920.
[35]*Ibid.*, November 15, 1920.

on the oil producers of the state. It is worthy to note, however, that during his two final terms Johnson introduced his two most significant pieces of legislation—the Livestock Commission Act of 1921 and the Johnson "Blue Sky Law" of 1923.[36]

Sam E. Johnson, Jr., had long been concerned about the wide latitude of action enjoyed by the livestock commission men of Texas, and late in the regular session of the legislature in 1921 he and Senator R. M. Dudley introduced and pushed through the legislature a Livestock Commission Bill which was to be described as a "piece of practical and safeguarding legislation which the cattle-growers of Texas have desired for many years." In essence the law provided: (1) that livestock commission houses must give bond double their daily business based on the average daily sales throughout the year 1920 and (2) that the commission men must remit payments to farmers and ranchers within forty-eight hours of the sale, Sundays and holidays excepted. It is of significance that, as the Blanco County *Record* reported, prior to the Johnson law, which passed the legislature in early March, no bond had been required and commission men took over the cattle by sending personal checks, some of which did not clear for two weeks. During the interval between purchase and payment, the commission men had the use "of the money for which checks were out" and anyone of a dishonest intent might "have imposed on the livestock selling public." As a result of his good work Sam Johnson received congratulatory messages from stockmen all over Texas and a special invitation to attend the cattle-raisers convention in San Antonio as an honored guest. His colleagues in the House of Representatives claimed that passage of the bill "at this late hour was a great victory for Representative Johnson."[37]

In an effort to curb abuses in the sale of securities, Johnson introduced his famous "blue sky law" in 1923 and pushed it through the legislature. Designed to protect the people of Texas from the sale of worthless securities, the Johnson law implemented an act of 1913 by creating the securities division of the Railroad Commission and extending the coverage of the earlier law. Having as its objective the stopping of "wholesale swindling which was being practiced by oil promoters and other stock-fraud special-

---

[36]H. J., 37th Legislature, 219f; 38th Legislature, 838, 1114, 395, 838.

[37]Blanco County *Record*, March 11, 1921.

ists," the law applied to "every person, broker, agent, joint stock company, co-partnership or organization, both foreign and domestic." It required "securing a permit to sell stock, application for which had to show the name under which the stock was to be sold, the name and address of each trustee plus other pertinent information about the trustees." All agreements under which business was to be conducted were to be made public. The par value of stock to be sold, its sale price, commissions to be paid, amount of stock to be issued, and promotion costs were to be shown. A detailed statement showing assets and liabilities, together with profits and losses, was to be filed with the securities division of the Railroad Commission. The law also required that advertising matter be filed with the division and the truthfulness of it sworn to. Finally the law provided checks on mergers, punished newspapers for false advertising regarding stock, limited the sale of stock on credit, and allowed the chief of the securities division to issue booklets or news releases warning the public of fraudulent stock.[38] The Johnson "blue sky law" marks a milestone in the history of state regulation of public securities.

Always interested in good roads, Sam E. Johnson continued to push for highway construction. In 1921 he gave valuable assistance to a drive which ultimately restored federal aid for two proposed highways in Blanco County. While Blanco-Johnson City residents appealed their case in mass, the *Record* reported that "had it not been for the diplomacy and good judgment of our representative, Hon. S. E. Johnson, Blanco County would probably have been delayed indefinitely in building her two highways." The following summer Johnson, "an enthusiastic good roads man," accompanied Judge Clarence Martin to Johnson City's Withers Opera House, where Martin made a speech picturing the advantages to be derived from good roads and urging "the necessity of voting additional bonds" for road construction. It is of considerable import that during the formative years of the Texas Highway Department, Sam E. Johnson, Jr., joined the vanguard in pushing the then infant highway program.

Throughout his public career, Johnson pushed the cause of the Confederate veterans, their widows, and dependents. It is apparent that he traveled thousands of miles at his own expense to

---

[38]*Ibid.*, January 26, 1923, p. 1.

obtain depositions establishing a pension claim for hundreds of widows of Civil War veterans. In this regard he was equally interested in state pensions for retired Texas Rangers. This interest in the welfare of others is the prime characteristic of Johnson's long and distinguished career as a public servant, a career that ended when he did not stand for re-election in 1924.

5

Looking back over the years, the residents of the Texas Hill Country remember Sam Ealy Johnson, Jr., with great admiration and fondness. Ava Johnson Cox, of Johnson City, recalls that her earliest memories of her Uncle Sam Johnson's political career came during his campaign for the state legislature in 1918; in reconstructing her vision of his appearance at that time, she reports that her attention was attracted "by his Stetson hat and his four-in-hand tie, as it was called in those days, and a high collar. His collar was very stiff and he was erect and impressive as he said, 'It is high time that a person stands up and lets the world know how he stands'—and Uncle Sam did just that."[39] Mr. Percy T. Brigham, Blanco banker and lawyer, simply says, "Mr. Sam was straight as a shingle. He represented his people well. I liked Sam Johnson." [40] Mr. J. R. Buckner, of Blanco and San Marcos, mentions the fact that Sam E. Johnson was "a big man in the Stetson-hat era of Texas politics"[41] and summarizes the significance of Johnson's career as follows:

I remember Mr. Sam as an outstanding man in his environment and in his time. He was a striking man in appearance; he was a grown man from the time I first remember him—a man who was interested in politics and also in legislation, especially for country people. Mr. Sam was a good conversationalist; he enjoyed the company of other men and always had something interesting to contribute that he had on his mind and that he was concerned about, and he was a pretty good entertainer. He was a good talker and I remember him as a man—as I say—that always was interested in some matter that concerned his community or his people. He was not a long distance poli-

---

[39] Alva Johnson Cox to W. C. P., August 14, 1964.

[40] Percy T. Brigham to W. C. P., July 8, 1964.

[41] "Stetson-hat era" is a reference to the fact that in the early decades of the Twentieth Century, a Stetson hat was the item most frequently involved in election betting.

tician, he was a politician of the area in which he lived, and his primary concerns were with those people in that area.

He was on the job all the time. Mr. Sam, as I remember him, was an unselfish person; a hard-working man. I remember even in his latter days he was much of the time away from home concerned with the interests of the state, and from the time I first knew him until towards the end of his career he was a man that was always busy about some state business.

Mr. Sam was a liberal man and he spent so much of his time and concern for the people of this area that he sometimes was said to have neglected his own business and he never became a well-to-do man because of that. I should say that if he had devoted his energies to his own well-being that he had the ability and the connections to make money, but he didn't do it. He gave his time and effort to his people. Mr. Johnson grew up in the ranching country and had that at heart all his life, and indulged somewhat in farming and ranching but I would say that his first love was politics; his first love was the concern that he had, the interest that he had in Austin through the legislature, in working for the interest of causes—causes that he felt were right. And he wanted to contribute to these causes.[42]

In agreement with the Buckner statement above, Mrs. Stella Glidden, newspaper editor and postmistress at Johnson City, remembers that

Mr. Johnson was one of the finest men I've ever known; he was a man whose entire life was devoted to the service of others. With neither selfish ends nor personal aggrandizement in mind, he gave his energies and talents to the cause of bettering the lot of his fellow man; if he had a dollar that he knew a friend needed, he would gladly give to the person whose need was greater than his; he never turned his back on a friend; he was the most unselfish man I've ever seen. No telling how much of his own money he spent in securing state pensions for Confederate veterans and their widows.[43]

But it remained for the woman who knew him best to give posterity a fair, honest, and accurate appraisal of her husband's political philosophy; years after Sam Johnson's death and a few years before the end of her own fruitful life, Rebekah Baines Johnson wrote:

He was ambitious, not so much for his own success as for that of his friends and his children, being alert to the interests of a loved one

---

[42]J. R. Buckner to W. C. P., September 12, 1964.

[43]Mrs. Stella Glidden to W. C. P., August 26, 1964.

and persistent in the promotion of the same. In his own advancement, he was retiring and modest.

He had a fine sense of organization and always thought out carefully the problems confronting him in the fields of his varied activities, determining the desired solution or goal, and then devising with ingenuity and ability the best and most economical means for acquiring the desired result. He always completely mastered a line of work before undertaking it. His judgment of men was almost infallible, and his decision regarding issues and underlying motives was discerning and acute.

He had a sound and sage philosophy which he expressed by a quoted axiom, proverb, or Scriptural passage. He liked to illustrate a situation by relating a remembered incident in history, a humorous anecdote, or a personal experience. He was an interesting conversationalist with a broad knowledge of state and national affairs, political figures and issues, and a deep understanding of people, their ideas, capacities, and desires. He delighted in being of service to those in need, giving sympathy and practical aid freely. Small wonder that "The House by the Side of the Road" was a favorite of his, as he was truly "a friend to man," extending hospitality to the truck driver who broke down in front of his door as graciously as to the Governor of the State who dropped in to talk politics.

Highly organized, sensitive, and nervous, he was impatient of inefficiency and ineptitude and quick to voice displeasure; equally quick, however, in making amends when some word of his caused pain to another. He was the most forgiving of men when an injury had been done to him, making excuses for the offender and completely forgetting the offense. . . . To those who knew him best, great heart seems best to describe him.[44]

Turning his back on another term in the state legislature in 1924, Sam Ealy Johnson ended his service to the public in that year except for an appointive term with the Motor Transport Division of the Railroad Commission, a position which he held during the early 1930's. After several years in residence at San Marcos, where their children attended Southwest Texas State College, Sam and Rebekah Johnson returned to their home in Johnson City in the fall of 1934 "to grow old together, quietly and happily." But not many years of happiness remained. The discovery of a serious heart condition was followed by a critical illness in 1935. His final days were spent in suffering and pain, and the end of life came on October 23, 1937. His beloved Rebekah found it difficult "to believe that the brilliant mind, the

---

[44]Rebekah Baines Johnson in Rebekah Johnson Bobbitt's Scrapbook.

dynamic personality, the great and loving heart of Sam Johnson were forever stilled. It is hard to undo the clasp of a hand that has held yours thro' all the trials and triumphs of thirty years." He was buried in the family cemetery on the banks of the Pedernales River on the following Sunday; during the final rites his friend Lon Smith said, "He was a man. Take him for all and all, I shall not look upon his like again."[45]

Thus it was that an old Democrat, worn by a modest but distinguished service to his state, found rest beneath the sturdy live oaks that border the waters of the Pedernales in his beloved Hill Country. Perhaps Sam Ealy Johnson, Jr., can be best described as an agrarian progressive who built upon the liberal traditions of American history to carve a place for himself in the political history of Texas. He consistently advocated legislation that calls attention to the fact that his political thinking was far in advance of that of the great majority of his contemporaries. His vision was far-sighted instead of provincial. His uncommon sympathy for the poor and unfortunate, combined with his desire for unselfish service to the causes of his fellow man, mark the broad extent of his humanitarianism. His tolerance of minority groups tended to set him apart from the majority of his fellow Texans of any generation. His early advocacy of economic regulatory measures and of state and national assistance to the needy (whether for individuals or for public and private agencies) label him as a pioneer in the welfare-state concept of the science of government. It may be said, therefore, that Sam Ealy Johnson represents a span in the political bridge that marks the course of American liberalism from the agrarian crusaders of the 1890's through Wilson's New Freedom to the New Deal days of Franklin D. Roosevelt—and, fortunately, beyond.

Not the least of Sam and Rebekah Johnson's achievements lies in the fact that they provided a warm home environment for their five children—the oldest of whom was destined to be the thirty-sixth President of the United States; it is now time to turn our attention to this important part of the story.

---

[45]*Ibid.*

III.

HOME AND SCHOOL

1

WHEN SAM E. JOHNSON, JR., MARRIED REBEKAH BAINES IN August of 1907, he took his bride to the old family homestead, a small tract of land on the north bank of the Pedernales River between the communities of Hye and Stonewall in Gillespie County. The Johnsons set up housekeeping in a low frame house with a porch or gallery across the front. Theirs was the typical farm home found in all rural areas of Texas during the early decades of the twentieth century.

Sam E. Johnson, Jr., was a good farmer and rancher and managed to make a living both on the farm and in Johnson City;

but partially as the result of severe financial losses in the cotton market in 1906, and partially because of the harsh nature of the rocky soil of the Pedernales valley, he never made money from either his efforts on the farm or, later, as a small-town real estate dealer. It was through the good financial management of Sam and Rebekah Johnson that a meager cash income was made to go a long way in covering the essential needs of a young and growing family. In this respect the Johnson family was typical of the tens of thousands of family farmers of the rural areas of Texas.

While Sam Johnson improved the house, set out the orchard, and tended the vegetable garden, Rebekah made the adjustments necessary to a happy marriage. Remembering these experiences on the farm, she wrote:

Normally the first year of marriage is a period of readjustment. In this case I was confronted not only by the problem of adjustment to a completely opposite personality, but also to a strange and new way of life, a way far removed from that I had known in Blanco and Fredericksburg. My early experiences on the farm were recently relived when I saw "The Egg and I"; again I shuddered over the chickens and wrestled with a mammoth iron stove. However, I was determined to overcome circumstances instead of letting them overwhelm me. At last I realized that life is real and earnest and not the charming fairy tale of which I had so long dreamed. This was the beginning of thirty years of married life, thirty busy beautiful years engaged in making a living and rearing five wonderful children who consumed our energies, our hopes and plans.[1]

On August 27, 1908, a year and a week after their wedding day, Sam and Rebekah Johnson's first child was born. A neighbor, Mrs. Christian Lindig, was summoned to attend the delivery of the baby. The young parents named their new son Lyndon Baines Johnson; and according to a cherished Pedernales valley story, a proud grandfather rode through the countryside to announce to the neighbors that "a United States Senator was born today, my grandson."

Lyndon Baines Johnson spent his earliest years on the family farm near Stonewall, in the midst of a family that always participated in the mainstream of life. With the aid of alphabet blocks, Mrs. Johnson taught her young son his ABC's before his third birthday. It is of great significance that the young boy enjoyed

---

[1]Rebekah Johnson in Rebekah Bobbitt's Scrapbook.

reading long before he was old enough to attend school. Under the watchful eye of his mother, he read from Anderson's and Grimm's Fairy Tales, Bible stories, Mother Goose rhymes, and, later, the poetry of Longfellow and Tennyson. Rebekah Johnson's great interest was in her son's education. An excellent teacher, she would, later on, take young Lyndon to school, and, "on the way, talk about history, geography, or algebra, giving him a kind of walking refresher course."[2]

Lyndon B. Johnson's formal education began in 1912 at the age of four, when, accompanied by his cousins, Ava and Margaret Johnson, he rode horseback for several miles to enroll at the Junction school—a one-room, one-teacher school near Stonewall. By the time the school term of 1913 came around, Sam and Rebekah Johnson had moved their growing family to Johnson City. Their home in town was a rambling frame house on the north side of a block-sized lot; the well, water tank, and out-buildings were located to the rear of the house. With the exception of a period of about two years immediately following the first World War, when the Johnson family again tried farming the old family homestead near Stonewall (as one of the children recently remarked: "Just long enough for daddy to go broke"), Lyndon Johnson attended the Johnson City schools from 1913 until his graduation in the spring of 1924. Recalling these tender years, he remembers that "My Daddy and my dear Mother were equally affectionate, equally considerate with their children, and we responded in kind. When I was not prepared with my studies, Daddy and Mother both stayed up with me until they were satisfied that I had mastered the assigned subject. I looked at them with equal respect and cherished them with identical love."[3]

By the time the family moved to Johnson City in 1913, Sam and Rebekah had become the parents of two additional children —Rebekah and Josefa. Shortly after the move another son, Sam Houston Johnson, was born; about two years later Lucia, the last of the children, arrived to brighten the Johnson home. Dur-

---

[2]Bruce Kowert, "Lyndon B. Johnson, Boy of Destiny," Boston *Globe,* December 15, 1963; Bela Kornitzer, "President Johnson Talks about His Mother and His Father," *Parade,* January 5, 1964.

[3]Kornitzer, "President Johnson Talks about His Mother and Father"; Gene Waugh, *Texas Public Employee* (March, 1964).

ing the years in Johnson City, Sam Johnson dealt in real estate and cattle as he kept a close eye on the local political scene.

By all odds, Lyndon B. Johnson, his brother, and his sisters spent a happy childhood. At this time, most of the entertainment was of the family variety. The barns, often serving as both garage and barn for the Johnson City families, provided the favorite play areas for the young children of the neighborhood. In this regard the Johnson home had an added attraction. Several years earlier Sam Johnson had traded for a place that had a small house on it; he moved the house into town and placed it on his lot to serve as a guest house. Of course, the Johnson guest house was preferable to a barn as a play area. The barns, however, were entirely adequate, especially after the fall harvest when each barn in the neighborhood would be filled with fresh peanut hay.

Other entertainment of Johnson City youngsters included riding horseback and working on nearby farms and ranches on weekends and during the summer vacation. Often on Saturday or Sunday afternoons, the boys of the community would gather on a vacant lot, or on the Johnson City baseball diamond, for intratown baseball games. The lanky young Lyndon Johnson excelled as a first baseman in these sandlot frays. It is reliably reported that, as he grew older, Johnson became a skillful fielder and hitter on the Johnson City school team.

In the days of his youth Lyndon B. Johnson was one of the local marble champions. In fact, he became so skillful at marbles that those who played the game with him four decades and more ago say that even today they would be reluctant to challenge him because they are sure that he would win easily.

Sometimes the Johnson youngsters and their friends mixed work and fun. Recalling some of the difficulties of life on the farm, Ava Johnson Cox tells the following story:

Uncle Sam and my father had a ranch down below Johnson City together and there were 85 acres that were in cultivation; on Saturday if we worked real hard and got the cotton picked out, we were all treated to home-made ice cream. Truman Fossett—the druggist—was our cousin, and he was working with us; in fact, Papa gathered up all the town children he could to help pick the cotton, and Cora Mae Arrington, Dave Arrington, and Mrs. Leonard—now superintendent of the schools—and Lyndon and Tom Crider, Otto Crider—there were some eighteen children. My mother did the cooking; she weighed the cotton out. She did the ramrodding, and Papa carried it to the gin. One day Lyndon and Tom and Otto and Ealy and Truman Fossett decided they would outpick all the girls in cotton—that's what Papa wanted—he got up a wager so he would be sure to get this bale of cotton out. In place of taking their nap at noon, Lyndon and Ealy and Tom and Otto and Truman all decided they would go back to the field real early, and we took our rest as usual. Well, on the way out there they got to betting who could ride the steers that Papa had in the patch—trap as we called it then, feeding trap—who could ride the most; . . . they got all wound up on who could ride the calves best, the steers rather, so they got to riding there and never reported to the cotton patch until four o'clock that afternoon, and they were automatically cut out of the ice cream supper that night. But anyway their intentions were good, but the girls won the ice cream supper. . . . Truman and I were talking about it the other day—he never did get to the cotton patch that afternoon; they rode calves and, of course, they were pretty well skinned up.[4]

Another pastime the youngsters enjoyed was to hitch a horse or donkey to a cart owned by Milton Barnwell and ride down to the Pedernales River for a picnic or an afternoon of swimming. They often had so much trouble keeping the cart in repair—apparently breakdowns were frequent—that they spent more time on their way to the river than they had for fun after arriving at their destination. And then there are the stories about the donkey. J. R. Buckner recalls seeing young Lyndon Johnson riding the donkey, or Mexican *burro*, at the Sunday baseball games between Johnson City and Blanco. Gene Barnwell Waugh reports that the animal belonged to Louis Rountree, while Ava Johnson Cox recalls that "it was the town donkey, and it was owned by Milton Barnwell, the doctor's son, and Louis Rountree." According to reliable sources, the boys took their donkey to baseball games and picnics, and they would ride the animal for ten or twenty-five cents a fall. Ava Johnson Cox remembers that "Lyndon had pretty good long legs and he would ride that donkey all evening long for ten cents a fall."[5]

During his formative years, Lyndon Johnson was fond of dogs and of hunting. In this regard Ava Johnson Cox relates:

He has always been a dog lover and long as I can remember he has

[4]Ava Johnson Cox to W. C. P., August 14, 1964.
[5]*Ibid.*; Gene Waugh in *Texas Public Employee;* J. R. Buckner to W. C. P., September 12, 1964.

always had hound dogs, or a dog of some kind. Of course, in those days we had hound dogs and in the winter time we would have what they called a trap line, and we'd run those traps and get the pelts and sell them for—well, Mr. Casparis bought everything we had; lots of times the furs were not prime and—as we would call them—they were blue hides, but he'd buy them from us just the same. Lyndon's old hound dog—old Evelyn as we called her—was the one we took on these hunts. Well, Evelyn had some baby pups one time, and he didn't know exactly what he was going to do about getting rid of these pups, and he didn't want them killed; so he fixed him up a sign and he put it in the barbershop window—"See me first for hound pups" and so he got rid of all of them. "See me first for hound pups, Lyndon B. Johnson"—he has always been a fast mover, got anything he wanted.[6]

During the summer months young Lyndon Johnson frequently joined Milton Barnwell and others at the croquet court in Dr. J. F. Barnwell's yard. The entire community, young and old, attended the Masonic suppers held during the fall and winter months at the Old Opera House in Johnson City. Both the croquet court and the "suppers" provided entertainment for the youthful residents of a small Hill Country town.

As the Johnson City youngsters became older, one of their favorite entertainments was the Saturday night dances. Always community affairs that were attended by entire families, these country dances were either parties held in a home or public affairs held in the larger dance halls at nearby Stonewall, Hye, Twin Sisters, or other rural communities.

Some of these community parties featured the German folk dances that were both typical and traditional in the German-American areas of Texas; on other occasions, however, the dancing followed the traditional patterns brought to Texas at an earlier date by the Anglo-American pioneers. The latter, perhaps best described as country and western dances—often square dances—featured music by a country string band that comprised a fiddle, one or more guitars, and sometimes a banjo. It was these Blanco and Gillespie county country dances, followed by similar experiences as a college student at San Marcos, that gave Lyndon B. Johnson an appreciation for American country music.

---

[6]Ava Johnson Cox to W. C. P., August 14, 1964.

Rebekah Baines Johnson

2

Growing up in the Sam Johnson home also had its serious side. When Sam E. Johnson left home to attend a legislative session in Austin, he would gather his children around him and remark: "Lyndon, I'm putting you in charge of things while I'm gone. See that all the chores get done and help mama all you can." Saddled with the responsibility of supervising the home, young Lyndon would then delegate the various chores to his brother and his sisters—such duties as chopping stove wood, filling the kitchen wood box, feeding the chickens, gathering the eggs, feeding the pigs, and tending to the needs of the horses and the cows. Of course, Lyndon would offer his help each day where it was most needed.

With a busy husband who was frequently away from home on public business, Rebekah Baines Johnson became a tower of strength to her young children. In a tribute to the sterling character of Mrs. Johnson, J. R. Buckner recalls: "I have heard praises of Mrs. Johnson since the time when I was a child. I also knew her after she moved to San Marcos, and I have never seen a mother more devoted to the interests and the welfare of her family. . . . There was never a mother that contributed more or was more concerned for the welfare of her family than was Mrs. Johnson." Speaking of her aunt, Ava Johnson Cox recalls, "Aunt Rebekah knew people better than Uncle Sam or Lyndon ever thought about knowing. She could read you like a book; she was a wonderful person."[7]

In addition to her interest in her family, Rebekah Baines Johnson was involved in almost every phase of community life in Johnson City. She often directed community plays in the Old Opera House, a building that served as the first courthouse in Johnson City until the new county courthouse was built. At that time Sam E. Johnson acquired ownership of the building, and it was here that he had his real estate office. It was in a portion of the same building that Harold Withers operated the town's silent movie, hence the name "Opera House." In addition to directing the community dramatic efforts, Mrs. Johnson taught public speaking, then termed "expression lessons," in her home. Gene Barnwell Waugh remembers "these lessons were the highlights of my young life. She was teaching me to recite rather long poems for banquets in Miss Tiny Spaulding's hotel long before I learned either to read or write. This was a credit to Mrs. Johnson. . . . I was only one of several 'inspired' young orators she taught."[8] While never a member of the public school faculty, Mrs. Johnson spent many hours coaching high school students in debate, ex-

---

[7]J. R. Buckner to W. C. P., September 12, 1964; Ava Johnson Cox to W. C. P., August 14, 1964.

[8]Gene Waugh in *Texas Public Employee.*

temporaneous speaking, and declamation in preparation for the county and district contests of the Texas Interscholastic League.[9]

These lessons in speech were given "in a room to the right of the entrance hall of the Johnson home," a room furnished with comfortable chairs and bookcases along each wall. Gene Waugh remembers that "Mrs. Johnson was seldom without one of those books in hand. . . . She was constantly finding new ways to interest her children and their friends, as well as her pupils, in the learning process."[10] It is quite evident, therefore, that Lyndon, together with Sam Houston, Rebekah, Josefa, and Lucia Johnson, was guided in his quest for knowledge by a devoted, sympathetic mother.

While Rebekah Johnson assumed the primary responsibility for the general education of her five children, Sam Ealy Johnson taught his sons the political facts of life. As a result, as Senator Ralph W. Yarborough has expressed it, Lyndon B. Johnson "grew up in a home in which government and politics were a part of the daily living; as everyday a subject as the weather is in a farm family. He learned at an early age to forecast political climate."[11] Later on, during his college days, going home for the Thanksgiving holidays meant to Lyndon Johnson "eating Mother's turkey and basking in her smiles and talking politics with Dad."[12]

President Johnson frankly admits that he learned his Democratic allegiance from a father who "went broke three times during Republican administrations" and who was so fiercely loyal to the Democratic Party that he named his horses for presidents— the good ones for Democrats and the sorry ones for Republicans. As the years passed, Sam E. Johnson also bequeathed to his growing son the qualities of political leadership. Three frequently told stories point out that Sam E. Johnson used to say, "if you couldn't come into a room full of people and tell right away who was for you and who was against you, you had no business in politics"; that the father used to wake his young son up in the morning by shaking the boy's leg and saying, "Get up, Lyndon, every boy in town already has a thirty-minute head start on you";

[9]*Ibid.;* Ava Johnson Cox to W. C. P., August 14, 1964.

[10]Gene Waugh in *Texas Public Employee.*

[11]*Congressional Record,* Proceedings of 87th Congress, 2d Session, p. 6210.

[12]*The College Star* (San Marcos), November 23, 1927.

and that the older Johnson advised, "When you're talking, you ain't learnin' nothin'."[13]

Aside from the mastery of the vital economic and political issues confronting the American people during the 1920's, it was from the close observation of the political activities of an ambitious, restless father that Lyndon Johnson learned the techniques of winning political allies and holding their allegiance; he also came to understand the value of an iron-clad political organization based on a delicate system of checks and balances regarding political debts and credits, the fine art of compromise, and a subtle knowledge of the many problems related to the planning of a successful political campaign. In all of these essentials Sam E. Johnson was a wise political counselor and young Lyndon a willing student.

In a recent work on the thirty-sixth President, Harry Provence reports that Lyndon B. Johnson remembers one morning long ago when a friend came to confide in his father at the Johnson home, "bearing word that it appeared as though seventy close-knit German votes in a nearby valley were going over to the other side in the next election." According to the story, "Sam Johnson, calm as always, told the friend to visit the head of this German clan and say that, on account of the incumbent county judge's ill health, folks were thinking that this worthy German would be the logical man to become county judge before long." The message was delivered (to the surprise of the recipient); and, when the votes were counted on election day, the seventy votes in that particular valley went to Sam E. Johnson—as he knew they would. Needless to say, young Lyndon was quick to see the political wisdom of this simple vote-getting technique.[14]

Young Johnson's desire to master the art of politics is no better illustrated than by the fact that Johnson City natives remember that as a youngster he would forego participation in childhood games to hang around the fringes of a circle of his elders and listen as they discussed local, state, and national politics. During the years between 1918 and 1924, a teen-age Lyndon Johnson accompanied his father on campaign trips (and other journeys re-

[13]Bruce Kowert, "Lyndon B. Johnson, Boy of Destiny," Boston *Globe*, December 15, 1963.

[14]Harry Provence, *Lyndon B. Johnson, A Biography* (New York, 1964), 31.

lated to political matters) as the elder Johnson worked to retain his seat in the Texas House of Representatives. Traveling in the family Model-T Ford, father and son stumped the county fairs, picnic grounds, church ice-cream suppers, and main-street political rallies in all of the towns and rural communities of Kendall, Blanco, Gillespie, and Llano counties. It is little wonder, therefore, that when Lyndon Johnson arrived at the campus of Southwest Texas State College a few years later to make up credits preparatory to college entrance, one of his teachers, when he read young Johnson's essay on current politics, exclaimed, "I didn't really believe that a boy so young could have had such a wide grasp of politics."[15]

As the result of this close association with his father and admiration for him, by the time Lyndon Johnson finished school in Johnson City and enrolled at Southwest Texas State College, his basic political ideals were taking shape. As associate editor of the *College Star,* Johnson urged his fellow students to "higher ideals" in a series of well-written editorials. It is of considerable significance that he had already formed definite opinions on such vital concepts as (1) the basic adaptability of the Constitution of the United States, (2) the tenets of American democracy, and (3) a vision of political liberalism as the central expression of the American democratic faith. These formative concepts, grounded in the high idealism of youth, are of such significance to the people of the United States today that it would be well, even at the risk of diversion from the main theme, to take a closer look at this aspect of young Johnson's life.

On September 17, 1927—Constitution Day—Lyndon Baines Johnson, then a second-year college student, commented on the 140th anniversary of the completion of the Constitution of the United States by pointing out that "this wonderful work is today the oldest written constitution still functioning" and "despite the tremendous changes time has brought, a great increase in population and expansion of territory, and marvelous advancement in various fields of learning and invention, the Constitution today justifies the prediction of the great William Pitt when he said, 'It will be the wonder and admiration of all future genera-

15*Ibid.*

tions and the model of all future generations'." Continuing, Johnson wrote:

The clearly defined plan of government outlined in the constitution by the fifty-five great students of political thought is at once practical as well as purposeful. The deliberations of these superior and courageous minds for four months finally achieved a plan for the carrying out of the purposes set forth in the preamble of the constitution. From the beginning to end it is a concise, harmonious, comprehensive, and thoroughly satisfactory, indeed wonderful, document. Although the Constitution is the basis of our government, and is generally conceded to be the wisest plan of government ever formulated; although we realize that our advancement as a nation under its rule has been remarkable, wholly unequalled in the history of nations; and although our phenomenal progress in science, invention, learning, commerce, art, education and statesmanship may be directly attributed to the vision and foresight of the constitution, we are, alas, shamelessly ignorant of the great principles of this matchless paper. The citizens of the United States know very little of the Constitution. This is a deplorable fact which should be remedied by careful study of this great work. Many lawyers know little of the Constitution. Occasionally a Joe Bailey may be found who devotes time and thought to the study of the constitution and who rises rapidly, not only in the legal profession, but in the political life of our nation.[16]

It is of considerable importance that, as a college student, Lyndon Johnson essentially agreed, perhaps unconsciously, with the great John Marshall, who, over a century before, while writing on the scope of the powers of the federal government in the famous case of *McCulloch v. Maryland,* concluded that "this provision of legislative power is made in a constitution intended to endure for ages to come, and consequently, to be adapted to the various crises of human affairs. To have prescribed the means by which government should, in all future time, execute its powers, would have been to change entirely the character of the instrument, and give it the properties of a legal code. It would have been an unwise attempt to provide . . . for exigencies which, if foreseen at all, must have been foreseen dimly. . . ."[17]

With regard to the second basic concept, the tenets of American democracy, the ninth observance of Armistice Day prompted Johnson to remember those who made the supreme sacrifice in

[16]*The College Star* (San Marcos, Texas), September 23, 1927.
[17]*McCulloch-v-Maryland* 4 Wheaton 316 (1819).

the Great War; he called attention to the fact that it was a war to make the world safe for democracy, to honor law, and to end all wars:

By honoring our heroes, by upholding democracy, by reverencing our laws, and by promoting peace, we in a measure show ourselves striving to become worthy of the supreme sacrifices the war exacted. Losing sight of these things, we find ourselves unworthy of the glorious heritage those war heroes left us. Ours is the duty, the privilege, the God-given task to bear on the lighted torch. Let us fail not, for "to break faith" with those who sleep in Flanders fields would indeed be the deed of a craven and ignoble soul—carry on![18]

Thirdly, the roots of young Johnson's vision of political liberalism as the keystone of American democracy was well illustrated in an editorial pointing out that "Behind all constructive work is a vision, a dream, a plan. Without this the work would lack spirit, organization, and power. It is the great compelling force that puts forth the first effort of the worker that sustains him in discouragement and cheers him to a consummation of the task."[19] The commentary on vision came a few weeks after an earlier essay in which Johnson continued the general theme of the significance of liberalism as compared to the destructive nature of iconoclastic cynicism:

The cynic is one of the greatest destructive agents in the world today. The cynic tears down faiths, ideals, and institutions. He ruthlessly destroys faith, confidence, and trust, and has no substitute to place in their stead.

The cynic sees only the bad. He is a confirmed pessimist, with a sneering disbelief in even the existence of good. To the cynic honesty is stupidity; religion is hypocrisy; advancement means trickery; and kindliness deceit. For him virtues do not exist. The semblances of them parade like wolves in sheeps clothing, concealing sins of deepest dye beneath their snowy coverings. The heart is corrupt regardless of the issues that proceed from it. Such are the beliefs of the cynic.

Not the cynic, but the men of faith are responsible for the progress of humanity, the building of nations, and the creation of our great government. All constructive work has been the product of the men of faith and vision.

Iconoclasts have in some cases helped to blaze the trail; but, when the work of construction began, they were missing. For example, in

---

[18]*Ibid.*, November 16, 1927.
[19]*Ibid.*, February 1, 1928.

the great struggle of the Revolution two matchless leaders were Thomas Paine and B. Franklin. Paine was only a revolutionist and a destroyer. He had no faith to sustain him. He passed from the scene of action reviling the great Washington, preferring libertinism to liberty, and predicting the final downfall of the new nation.

Franklin was upheld by a great faith. He had something to replace the discarded government. He was a great constructor, a builder, a man of vision and faith. To him and his great compatriots belongs the credit for the existence of our great republic. These noble souls had faith in the cause of liberty which sustained them through seven long years of struggle, and a vision of a nation in which liberty, happiness, and opportunity should be the portion of the common people. Faith builds, but cynicism destroys.

While cynicism has a blighting effect upon all who come in contact with its exponents, it wields a very blasting influence on the individual cynics. Their souls are warped and twisted by their distorted ideas. A man is what he desires to be. If he cherishes noble, unselfish thoughts he will be a broadminded, liberal citizen, doing a constructive work of upbuilding and uplifting in the world. If he has a narrow cynical outlook on life, he will be an iconoclast, destroying old ideas and traditions, and establishing nothing in their places.[20]

Three decades later Lyndon Baines Johnson, then recognized as the Democratic Party leader in the United States Senate, again recorded the essential ideas that comprised his political philosophy. It is significant that on this more mature occasion Johnson underscored his basic philosophy by returning to John Marshall's "adaptative philosophy" of the Constitution by calling attention to the fact that "had America been bound by the Constitutional Convention to the philosophies of the eighteenth century—and by the limits of the wisdom and vision of these times— we would not have the nation that is ours today. Our rising greatness through more than 180 years has come from our freedom to apply our accumulating knowledge to the processes of self-government. Or, to state it another way, this has come because America's course has been left to the living. Thus, the eighteenth-century philosophy of our Constitution has allowed for growth so that it will be strong."[21]

Departing from this Constitutional foundation, Johnson pointed out that "It is a part of my own philosophy to regard indi-

---

[20]*Ibid.*, December 7, 1927.

[21]Lyndon B. Johnson, "My Political Philosophy," *Texas Quarterly* (Winter, 1963), 10.

viduality of political philosophy as a cornerstone of American freedom" and then proceeded to outline the tenets of his own political belief as follows:

First, I believe every American has something to say, and, under our system, a right to an audience.

Second, I believe there is always a national answer to each national problem, and, believing this, I do not believe that there are necessarily two sides to every question.

Third, I regard achievement of the full potential resources—physical, human, and otherwise—to be the highest purpose of governmental policies next to the protection of those rights we regard as inalienable.

Fourth, I regard waste as the continuing enemy of our society and the prevention of waste—waste of resources, waste of lives, or waste of opportunity—to be the most dynamic of the responsibilities of our government.

. . . Thus whatever we are to be we must build from those things at our disposal, and to content ourselves with less than the ultimate potential is to deny our heritage and our duty.[22]

Conceding that the above tenets were simple and personal, Lyndon B. Johnson concluded his philosophical essay, as he began, with the statement that he was "a free man, an American, a United States Senator, and a Democrat, in that order. . . ."[23] It is of the utmost significance to any person attempting to trace the evolution of President Johnson's personal political ideals that his basic philosophy was formed at an early age, has continued to be the driving force behind his distinguished political career, and has remained essentially unchanged over the years. As a young man, Johnson wrote of visions, dreams, responsibilities, duty, and "ultimate potentials"; over three decades later he is still writing of the same things. To a large extent these noble ideals were formulated as a youth around the hearth of the Johnson family home in Johnson City; they stand today as a monumental tribute to the combined character and lives of Sam Ealy and Rebekah Baines Johnson.

3

Returning to the young years in Johnson City and vicinity, perhaps we would do well to point out that Lyndon Johnson's

---

[22]*Ibid.,* 9.

[23]*Ibid.,* 11.

formative years included about as much work as play and study. During the difficult years following the first World War—years of agricultural depression when drudgery and toil against the unyielding rocks of the Texas hills blighted the human resources of the whole region—young Johnson found it necessary to work in order to have a few surplus dimes and quarters for spending money. As a result he shined shoes on afternoons after school and on weekends in the Johnson City barbershop. He also made spending money by working as "printer's devil" in the local newspaper shop; by herding cattle, goats, and sheep on nearby ranches; and, as noted previously, by working in the grain and cotton fields of both family and friends.

In spite of the necessity for work, school came first. All indications point to the fact that Johnson was an excellent student of a curious and inquiring mind; that he was a mischievous sort of youngster, always with a twinkle in his eye, a trait that sometimes got him into minor difficulties with teachers and school administrators, who traditionally lack a sense of humor in cases where exceptional students, seeking activity to occupy busy minds, occasionally run afoul of the rules of discipline; and that he was a well-rounded student who participated in the so-called extracurricular activities of the school (he excelled in public speaking, debate, and baseball).

By the spring of 1924 Lyndon B. Johnson, age fifteen, was in his last semester at Johnson City High School. As always, the last few months prior to graduation were busy ones for the students. At this time there were only ninety students in the entire Johnson City school system—and six comprised the roll of the senior class. In April, 1924, Lyndon Johnson and fourteen other students from Johnson City journeyed to San Marcos to take part in the district meet of the Texas Interscholastic League. Johnson and Johnnie B. Casparis won third place in debate, defeating an able Seguin team to win points for their school.[24] Young Johnson also found time to play baseball for the school team. Although newspaper reports of the baseball season are skimpy, one story related that in early March the Johnson City team boarded a truck and went "to the big flat opposite the Johnson Ranch on the Pedernales River" to play a team representing Albert and

---

[24]Blanco County *Record*, April 25, 1924.

Hye. Johnson City won the game 22-9, collecting 31 hits, and making 9 errors. Lyndon Johnson pitched and played first base in this contest. Other players on the Johnson City team included Ebling, Edwards, Tom Crider, Otto Crider, C. Stribling, R. Kennedy, W. Stevenson, B. Stevenson, and W. Crider.[25]

Graduation exercises for the class of 1924 were held on the evening of May 4. Lyndon Johnson read the class poem; and, according to the Blanco County *Record*, "Lyndon was one of the winners of the county debate this year, and has won honors in declamation in both the county and district. He is the youngest member of the class and is believed to be the youngest graduate of the school. He has a quick mind and a winning personality and has to his credit more units than are required for graduation."[26] Other members of the class of 1924 were Kitty Clyde Ross, Louise Casparis, John Dollahite, Margaret Johnson, and Georgia Cammack.

A few weeks after the close of the school term of 1924 Lyndon Johnson was not ready for a decision concerning college. He and five friends bought an automobile, pooled their cash, and set out for California, camping along the way. They reached their destination without encountering great difficulty; but when they started looking for work, they discovered that unskilled labor could not command much of a wage. During these difficult weeks, Lyndon Johnson washed cars, washed dishes in an eating establishment, and picked fruit in the orchards of the Imperial Valley —and came close, at times, to starvation. He returned home after several months on the West Coast and took a job on a highway work crew near home.

Preferring to work on the road gang rather than to attend college, although his mother constantly urged him to return to school, Johnson, like others of his generation, liked the small weekly wage that resulted from his labor. Mrs. Kitty Clyde (Ross) Leonard remembers:

. . . the President graduated from high school at the age of 15. He, like most 15 year old youngsters, had not matured enough to have a definite goal even though his parents had always wanted him to have a college education and had dreams of a successful career for him.

---

[25]*Ibid.*, March 4, 1923.

[26]*Ibid.*, May 9, 1924.

Today many boys of 18 have not made up their minds what they want to do after graduation. Many boys today go into service and then come back with a determination for a career. Lyndon Johnson, at 16, went to California. There he found that the world was not too kind to a person who was trained in no skill. Then, he returned to Johnson City and took a job with a highway construction company.

Now, perhaps it would be wise to think of highway construction forty years ago. Picks, shovels, sledge hammers, and fresnoes pulled by four mules made up the machinery for highway construction. It was this kind of work which he was doing for very low daily wages.

I really think that it was while he was on this job that the impact of all his parents' teachings and admonitions took on new importance and Lyndon Johnson "became of age." It was then that he determined to make the most of the talents and abilities with which God so liberally endowed him. He had a goal and worked with all his might to attain the goal.[27]

It is significant that young Lyndon Johnson never lost sight of the possibility of an eventual college education. As Johnson tells the story, he made his decision in late February, 1927, following a night on the town that ended in a fight. After a telephone call by a delighted mother to President C. E. Evans of Southwest Texas State College, Sam E. and Rebekah Johnson scraped together a few dollars for their son. Lyndon then went to Blanco to counsel with Mr. Percy T. Brigham of the Blanco bank. Brigham, a kindly man who understood the financial plight of youngsters in search of an education, made a small loan. Equipped with enough cash to cover the cost of enrollment, Johnson then hitchhiked to San Marcos to start his college career. He had passed another milestone in his young life.

---

[27]Kitty Clyde Leonard to D. E. C., April 6, 1965.

IV.

"THIS SCHOOL, MR. PRESIDENT, IS MY ALMA MATER"

I

THERE ARE HUNDREDS OF SMALL COLLEGES IN THE UNITED States like Southwest Texas State College, San Marcos, Texas. Year after year, these colleges graduate well-educated young men and women who become useful and prominent citizens, and yet the colleges do not achieve national reputations. Perhaps they remain obscure because they are so small or because there are so many of them, but it is the worst kind of intellectual snobbery to assume that gradutes of obscure colleges have inferior educations. Great modern universities are distinguished principally for their graduate, medical, and law schools, and for their research facilities. The quality of undergraduate instruction is not necessarily related to the size of the institution. Moreover, the advantages of small classes and individual attention to students at the smaller colleges are obvious.

A surprising fact about small colleges is that many of our presidents attended them. Most Americans know that some of our presidents graduated from great institutions like Harvard (both Adamses, both Roosevelts, and Kennedy); Princeton (Madison and Wilson); William and Mary (Jefferson, Monroe, and Tyler); and West Point (Grant and Eisenhower). Many also know that the White House has been occupied by a Yale man (Taft), a graduate of North Carolina (Polk), and a product of Stanford University (Hoover). Some people even know that one doctor of philosophy has been president—Woodrow Wilson (Johns Hopkins). But how many Americans know that presidential educations were also acquired at Bowdoin College of Maine (Pierce), Dickinson College of Pennsylvania (Buchanan), Kenyon College of Ohio (Hayes), Williams College of Massachusetts (Garfield), Union College (now University) of New York (Arthur), Miami College (now University) of Ohio (Benjamin Harrison), Amherst College of Massachusetts (Coolidge), and Southwest Texas State College (Lyndon Johnson)? Some of these are now large colleges and universities, to be sure; nonetheless, they were small when the future presidents attended them.

Certainly a college education is not a prerequisite for being president. Twelve of our presidents reached the White House without benefit of formal higher education (Washington, Jackson, Van Buren, William Henry Harrison, Taylor, Fillmore, Lincoln, Andrew Johnson, Cleveland, McKinley, Harding, and Truman). But most of these—all but Washington, Harrison, Johnson, Harding, and Truman—got their advanced education in law offices.[1]

If Harvard claims credit for educating the Adamses, the Roosevelts, and Kennedy, then Kenyon must be given credit for upright and sincere Rutherford B. Hayes, Union for promising but short-lived James A. Garfield, and Southwest Texas State College for Lyndon B. Johnson. A brief history of the

---

[1] James Morgan, *Our Presidents* (New York, 1949), 414-417.

President's alma mater seems appropriate, therefore, in any treatment of his formative years.

The college was not founded until the turn of the twentieth century. State universities and colleges had a rather slow start in Texas. Several private and church-sponsored colleges were established during the Republic and pre-Civil War days, but no state institutions of higher learning were founded. Suggestions had been made by governors and members of the state legislature that a state university be founded, but nothing was done. It was not until the passage of the Morrill Act of 1862 that the impetus came to establish the first state college in Texas. The Morrill Act provided federal land grants in aid for the purpose of establishing colleges to train students in the agricultural and mechanical arts. After the disruptions of the Civil War and Reconstruction period, Texas established its first land grant college, the Agricultural and Mechanical College at College Station. At the same time a land grant college for Negroes opened at Prairie View, though it closed within a year for lack of students.

About the same time, agents of the Southern Education Fund, an agency financed by philanthropist George Peabody, made a study of the needs for teacher training in Texas. On the basis of this study, the Fund made an offer of $12,000 to the state of Texas to finance the establishment of two normal or teacher-training schools. The state matched the $12,000 and in 1879 established Sam Houston Normal School at Huntsville and re-established Prairie View as a teacher-training school for Negroes. Later, in 1881, the legislature appropriated money for the foundation of a state university at Austin which opened its doors to students in 1883.

The success of the schools at Huntsville and Prairie View was enough to encourage Governor O. M. Roberts to recommend in 1881 the establishment of two more normal schools, one at San Marcos and one at Denton in North Texas. The legislature delayed until 1899, however, before enacting the recommendation into law. Even then that body did not provide sufficient money for opening the schools. The citizens of San Marcos, anxious to have their school start operation, held a public meeting in 1900 and petitioned the legislature to provide sufficient funds. Their appeal, couched in terms flowery enough to bring a blush from even the most ardent chamber of commerce booster, described San Marcos as a community "renowned for its beautiful river and healthful location, for its schools and churches, and the high moral tone of its citizenship." Most of the streets were well paved or macadamized; there were more than thirty mercantile establishments doing a "lucrative" business, and the town was served by two railroads.

Already, the city of San Marcos had donated as a site for the normal school a hill near town which had been used for Chautauqua meetings. The San Marcos petition described the site in glowing terms: "Near the head of the San Marcos River, and overlooking its meanderings, a cedar-crowned hill, whose beauty attracts the eye of every visitor . . . has been . . . donated as a site for this normal school." At the very foot of Chautauqua Hill was a federal fish hatchery which presented a picture of varied water and landscape scenery; when fully developed, the school would "have no rival in attractiveness and practical utility." Beyond the hatchery lay the beautiful San Marcos River, as "pure as a maiden's dream." The petition suggested that the bubbling headwaters of the river would symbolize the fountain of knowledge which was to be established on the hill nearby.[2]

Accordingly, in 1901, the legislature appropriated money to build a brick building on the eastern crest of Chautauqua Hill. That building, costing only $50,000, still stands and remains the most dominant feature of the campus and, indeed, of the surrounding countryside. With a red, high-pitched roof and numerous spires, peaks, and parapets, "Old Main," as it is now called, looks from a distance like a medieval castle. It can be seen from several miles by travelers approaching across the plains which lie to the east. Down through the years "Old Main" has come to occupy a key place in the hearts of students and faculty, and to tear it down or drastically remodel it would be unthinkable to them.

The law which created the Southwest Texas Normal School declared that such a school was needed in the southwest part of the state because distances were too great for students to travel to Sam Houston Normal at Huntsville. The purpose of the school was quite simple: to train teachers in the region.

---

[2] Announcement of the Southwest Texas State Normal School, 1903, pp. 8-9.

Operations began on September 9, 1903, making the school the sixth oldest institution of higher learning in Texas. North Texas State Normal School at Denton, which had been authorized at the same time as Southwest Texas, was able to begin operating as a state school in 1901 because a private school already existed there.

One of the first problems facing the school at San Marcos was choosing a name, and indeed throughout its sixty-five-year history it has been a school in search of a name. It began life in 1899 as "The Southwest Texas State Normal School" in keeping with the then current trend of establishing normal schools to train qualified public school teachers. In 1913 the school was made a junior college by the addition of two years of college work to the curriculum. In 1917 two more years at the college level were added, making Southwest Texas a senior college. In 1919 the name was changed to "Southwest Texas State Teachers College at San Marcos." Obviously, this was a lengthy and awkward name; moreover, it was not even descriptive. A quick look at a map of Texas will reveal that San Marcos is not in Southwest Texas. In the mid-decades of the nineteenth century, when the westward moving frontier barely included the eastern half of Texas, San Marcos was southwest of most of settled Texas; but today there is a great expanse of Texas which lies west of the city.

By most standards San Marcos is in South-Central or South Texas. The reader may be asking himself at this point just what difference it makes where San Marcos is, but the answer is that it makes a great deal of difference. There is no more similarity between East Texas and West Texas than between Louisiana and New Mexico. Likewise, Central and South Texas are distinctive. The Hill Country, where Lyndon Johnson was born, is the historic buffer zone between the long-settled farming country of Central Texas and the ranch country of West Texas. Since the college at San Marcos was largely a regional college, it seems important that it should have been named for the region it served—South-Central Texas—but this was not to be.

Most people, even students and graduates, despaired of keeping up with the official name changes of the school and called it simply "San Marcos," or "San Marcos State College"—a usage which Lyndon Johnson retains to this day. The "Teachers" was dropped from the name in 1961, but "Southwest Texas State College" still remains a mouthful, and everyone from news commentators to the newly inaugurated president of the college has trouble with it. The supreme outrage came when *Life* in 1964 characterized the school as "Southwest State Teachers, a Baptist school in San Marcos."[3] This bit of journalistic fiction took real creative thought; the reporter had to make up the whole name to make this error. It is true that there is a Baptist-supported institution in San Marcos; but it is San Marcos Academy, a secondary school. In addition, it is obvious that a school could not be a "State Teachers College" and a "Baptist supported institution" at the same time.

Some day the college will find a more suitable name. Maybe it will be "San Marcos State College," and it has even been suggested that it become "Lyndon B. Johnson State College." Since several other state colleges in Texas are named for former governors of the state, it does not seem impossible that one might be named for the only president from Texas.

Southwest Texas opened its doors in 1903 to 303 students. It was headed by Thomas G. Harris, former superintendent of schools in Dallas and Austin. Harris held two degrees from Carson-Newman College in Tennessee and was well-known in public school circles throughout the state. He assembled a faculty of six men and ten women and laid out a curriculum which included English, history, physics, mathematics, music, chemistry, geography, biology, Latin, German, and other subjects. In the next eight years Southwest Texas grew and prospered; enrollment doubled during the period and the future looked bright. Then President Harris ran aground on a rock that was to trouble the college several times during its history— political interference. While he was superintendent of schools in Dallas and Austin, Harris had edited a magazine called *The Texas School Journal*. As editor he had carried on a long campaign to get increased revenues for school districts and higher pay for teachers. On one occasion Harris was severely critical in his magazine of a state legislator named O. B. Colquitt, who

---

[3]*Life*, August 14, 1964, p. 77.

had made the rather intemperate remark on the floor of the House that "school teachers are not tax-payers but tax-eaters." Harris's subsequent criticism of Colquitt's remarks started a personal feud, and it came as extremely bad news to Harris that Colquitt was elected governor of Texas in 1910. Under heavvy pressure from the governor, the governing board of the college removed Harris as president.[4]

. *Cecil E. Evans*

Harris was replaced by Cecil E. Evans, who had been for

[4]John M. Smith, "The History and Growth of the Southwest Texas State Teachers College," master's thesis, Southwest Texas State College, 1930, pp. 26-31.

the previous three years General Agent for the Conference for Education in Texas. Evans held a B.A. degree from Oxford College in Alabama and a master's degree from the University of Texas. Later he was to receive an honorary LL.D. from Southwestern University in Georgetown, Texas. In his previous career Evans had been principal and superintendent of schools in several cities in Alabama and Texas. As General Agent for the Conference for Education, he had helped push through three state constitutional amendments for the benefit of public schools.

Evans became the most important figure in the history of the development of Southwest Texas State College. He was chiefly interested in improving the physical facilities, in upgrading his faculty, and in getting to know the students and keeping up with their careers after they left college to teach. He was proud of his college and proud of the teaching profession. According to one long-time faculty member, Dr. Evans's chief diversion was politics. Said M. L. Arnold, head of the History Department," . . . he has a wonderful insight into political situations and an equally notable capacity for detecting political trends." Arnold added that Evans had a remarkable memory for details of past political happenings and "wide acquaintance with the politics and politicians of the state."[5]

One of the better descriptions of President Evans was written in 1928 by the editor of the *College Star,* the student newspaper. The young editor, an ardent admirer of Evans and later to be quite close to him, was named Lyndon Johnson. He wrote that the advancement of Southwest Texas apparent in 1928 was the result in great part to "the ability, energy, and untiring zeal of Dr. Evans." He identified Evans as a "Democrat, Methodist, Member of N.E.A. [and] Mason." Johnson said that Evans possessed "lofty ideals, broad sympathies, intensity of purpose," and had devoted the "supreme efforts of his life" to the development of Southwest Texas. He continued:

Great as an educator and as an executive, Dr. Evans is greatest as a man. Here we find a man who cherishes a fellowship with the humanities of life. He plans for deeds that live, leaving indelible impress on the lives of the youth of the college. With depth of human sympathy rarely surpassed, unfailing cheerfulness,

[5]*Ibid.,* 36-37.

geniality, kind firmness, and friendly interest in the youth of the state, Dr. Evans has exerted a great influence for good upon the students of the S.W.T.S.T.C. He finds great happiness in serving others.[6]

Evans was a man of simple tastes and with few affectations. He lived in the plain house during his tenure as president, and upon his retirement he moved into a modest home from preference rather than necessity. On one occasion when a faculty member built a new home which was comfortable but not nearly as luxurious as the three-story houses of some of the downtown merchants, Evans remarked that faculty members had no business building fancy homes.

Ironically, Evans, who was a moderate man politically, was brother to Hiram Wesley Evans, Imperial Wizard of the Ku Klux Klan during the 1920's. Though Evans never spoke of the Klan or his brother, there were those on the campus and in town who thought he was pro-Klan, whereas others thought he was the opposite. Because of his refusal to commit himself, Evans was attacked politically by an older student of the college who was a Klansman. The student organized a campaign against him and enlisted the support of school superintendents in the region and several members of the board of regents. Eventually the storm blew over; but Evans took no disciplinary action against the student, perhaps out of fear of the Klan.[7]

Throughtout the early 1920's President Evans and his faculty worked to make Southwest Texas a fully accredited senior college. The main hurdle was the Southern Association of Colleges and Schools. Accreditation of a college is based on the training of its faculty, its library, its classroom and laboratory space, and its requirements for courses and degrees. The Southern Association had high standards; and after several years of seeking and not quite winning approval, President Evans told the Association, "You prescribe and we will do." It was done that way, and Southwest Texas became one of the first teachers colleges in the South to be fully accredited as a senior college.

In 1919 Evans brought the first holder of a doctorate degree to the faculty of the college. He was Alfred H. Nolle from the

[6]*College Star,* July 25, 1928, p. 1.
[7]Interview with Alfred H. Nolle, San Marcos, November 14, 1964.

University of Pennsylvania. Nolle was a professor of Germanic languages and in 1922 was made the first academic dean of the college. As dean he became the guardian of standards and scholarship, and under his leadership the academic life of the college grew and prospered. For many years Nolle was a member of the Committee on Standards of the Texas Association of Colleges and Universities, and later president of this organization. In these positions he took part in the accreditation of many Texas colleges and the academic liquidation of a few.

A biography which appeared in the *College Star* in 1928 and which might well have been written by Lyndon Johnson, since he was editor at the time, described Nolle as "mentally alert, experienced, specially trained, just, capable, and interested . . . a scholar, gentleman, and executive [who] is a strong and vital force in the upbuilding of S.W.T.T.C."[8] In 1959, when Nolle was nearing the end of his active career, Senate Majority Leader Lyndon Johnson rose from his desk on the aisle in the Senate chamber and said:

> Mr. President, after 40 years of service, Dr. Alfred H. Nolle is retiring this fall as dean of Southwest Texas State College at San Marcos, Texas.
> This school, Mr. President, is my alma mater.
> To me, as he has been to thousands, Dean Nolle was a guide, a counselor, a friend, and great inspiration.

The majority leader then had entered in the *Congressional Record* a story from a Texas newspaper of Nolle's retirement.[9]

In an earlier letter to Nolle, Senator Johnson wrote that his warmest memories centered around the college and San Marcos. He said:

> It was there that you and the rest of the faculty took a raw Hill Country boy and tried to make an educated man of me. To the extent that I have succeeded in life, I can claim that you were successful. But this was because no one could go through the school without absorbing some of your character and high standards of integrity.[10]

---

[8]*College Star*, July 25, 1928, p. 4.

[9]U. S. Congress, *Congressional Record*, 86th Cong., 1st Sess., August 20, 1959, pp. A7191-A7192.

[10]Lyndon B. Johnson to Alfred H. Nolle, April 10, 1957.

There were other faculty members of importance, some of whom will be discussed later. However, the principal ingredient of any college is the students. The young men and women who attended Southwest Texas in the 1920's came from similar backgrounds. They were what are called in South Texas "Anglos" or whites. Nearly all of them were from small towns and rural areas within a hundred miles of San Marcos. From the German settlements—towns like Seguin, New Braunfels, and Fredericksburg— which lie in a half-moon stretching through five or six counties to the south and west of San Marcos, came the German students with their barely perceptible accents. From the prairie farming communities with names like Lockhart, Luling, and Gonzales to the east and the smaller and more picturesque Hill Country towns to the northwest such as Blanco and Johnson City (also the home towns of many German-American students) came Anglo-Saxon types with their western garb and their Texas twang. There were youngsters of Czech, Polish, and Bohemian descent from towns to the southeast such as Hallettsville and Shiner. Others came from Gulf Coast towns like Port Lavaca and Aransas Pass, and quite a few came from the tropical citrus-growing lower valley of the Rio Grande—towns such as Mission, Edinburg, and Harlingen. The cities of Austin and San Antonio, which are close to San Marcos, were also liberally represented.

In South Texas there were three major ethnic groups: Anglos, Latin-Americans (people of Mexican descent), and Negroes. Only Anglos and some Latin-Americans went to college in the 1920's and 1930's. In earlier days there had even been discrimination against certain white groups, such as the Germans, Czechs, Poles, and Latins. After World War II Latins enrolled in larger numbers, and Negroes gained admittance by legal action in 1963.

By the late 1920's Southwest Texas had become a true regional college. It was primarily a teachers' college, to be sure; but many students attended who did not plan to be teachers and wanted only a college education. In this region Southwest Texas was "the college." If a youngster planned to go off to school, it was simply assumed that he would go to San Marcos. This was true in Blanco County, where Lyndon Johnson grew up. In 1927, when Johnson entered college, few from Blanco County had ever gone to the big univerity in Austin although it was only thirty or forty miles away. A few Baptists went to Baylor University in Waco and a few Methodists to Southwestern University at Georgetown, but most went to the college at San Marcos. In 1929, for instance, there were twenty-two students at Southwest Texas from Blanco County, a remarkable number from a county with a population of no more than 2,500.

One way Southwest Texas spread its influence in the region was through its teachers. Students like Lyndon Johnson went all the way through primary and secondary school being taught altogether by teachers trained in San Marcos. The chances were that their principals and superintendents were also graduates of the college. Southwest Texas offered two other attractions: It provided an excellent teacher-training program, and it was one of the least expensive colleges in the entire region. Tuition was nominal; local fees and deposits totaled only seventeen dollars per semester, including textbook rental. There were no college dormitories until the 1930's, but private boarding houses provided room and board for twenty-five or thirty dollars a month. Many young women—and a few young men—effected economies in living costs by doing "light housekeeping." Some students supported themselves in college by working in the homes of San Marcos families. Duties included cooking, cleaning, and caring for children; and advertisements for student help specified that girls must be experienced in domestic work and physically strong.[11]

It was possible for a student to come to Southwest Texas with no help from home and work his way through four years of schooling. President Evans had seen to that. It was his feeling that much talent was lost in America for lack of opportunity, and he was determined to provide a college where youngsters who really wanted an education could get it if they were willing to work. Evans's policy was to give students part-time employment wherever possible instead of filling positions with full-time employees. If a job could be done by one permanent employee, he would rather hire two or even three students to do it. As a result, students worked in the administrative offices, the library, the cafeteria, the book store, on the maintenance and construction crews, and as janitors and even as night watch-

---

[11]San Marcos *Record*, September 3, 1926, "Teachers College Section," 1.

men. In 1928 Lyndon Johnson wrote of Evans: "It was his delight to assist poor boys and girls to secure an education, and through his efforts many have been placed in positions where they could defray their expenses at school."[12]

A student making thirty dollars a month had to pay twenty-five of it for room and board. That left the munificent sum of five dollars for such incidentals as laundry, clothing, and entertainment. Some did without breakfast in order to have more money for other necessities. About fifty-five per cent of boys at Southwest Texas had some kind of job. Most of them could not have afforded an education at any other college. Typical of these was Clyde Nail, a boy who came to Southwest Texas in 1929 from his home in San Antonio with barely enough money to get to the campus. He worked on a construction crew for a while and then got a highly coveted job as a college carpenter. According to Nail, Southwest Texas was a "poor boy's school but a lot of fun." Like many other students of that time, he recalls his years on the Hill as "the happiest of my life." Today he says with deep feeling, "I will remain forever grateful to the college for those years and for the opportunity to get an education." Nail went on to graduate work at the University of Texas and eventually became vice-president of San Antonio College.[13]

In 1927, when Lyndon Johnson entered Southwest Texas there were ten buildings on the campus, plus shops, laboratories, gymnasiums, and athletic fields and courts. There were also three model schools in which the children of San Marcos were taught and a forty-acre demonstration farm. The library was small, only 21,000 volumes, but it was growing. There was a faculty of fifty-six, divided into departments of agriculture, biology, chemistry, economics, business administration, education, English, public speaking, art, music, history, geography, home economics, industrial arts, Latin, physics, mathematics, auto mechanics, modern languages, and physical training for men and women. The biggest department was English, with eight professors. Some departments had only one or two. Most of the faculty held master of arts degrees in their teaching field. Quite a few of

[12]*College Star*, July 25, 1928, p. 1.
[13]Interview with Clyde Nail, San Antonio, December 18, 1964.

them had been trained at George Peabody College for Teachers and Columbia University, both of which were highly respected as teacher-training institutions. Many of the faculty had graduated from the University of Texas and other well-known universities, such as Vanderbilt, Chicago, Missouri, California, and Michigan.

The college offered two degrees, a bachelor of science and a bachelor of arts, with majors in any of the various departments of the college. In addition, a sophomore diploma was given for successful completion of two years of college. Degree requirements were stiff; for instance, the bachelor of arts curriculum included twenty-seven term hours (three years) of foreign language. Other requirements included courses in the arts and sciences in addition to the major and minor courses. A "C" average was required for graduation. The college was on the quarter system, which meant that each school term was three months long. A degree required 180 term hours, or the equivalent of fifteen hours a week in class for four school years.

The courses offered at Southwest Texas were divided into introductory or survey courses, which were largely for freshmen and sophomores, and advanced courses. The advanced offerings in English, for example, included courses in Chaucer, Shakespeare, Milton, Restoration Drama, the Romantic Poets, Walt Whitman, and Victorian and Modern British poetry. As a service to future teachers, every department of the college taught at least one course in the methods of teaching its subject matter.[14]

Any judgment on the caliber of teaching at Southwest Texas is, of course, an intangible thing. Information from those involved in the school, whether as teachers or students, might be biased; and those not involved would not be in a position to know. Possibly the best source for an objective view would be a young instructor who came to the college from a large university and was therefore in a position to compare. Such a young instructor was Leland Derrick, who came to teach at the college in 1926 with a degree from the University of Texas. Derrick was told by President Evans that freshman instruction in English at South-

---

[14]The Southwest Texas State Teachers College, *Catalog for 1927-28*, XVI, No. 13, June, 1927.

west Texas would compare favorably with that of the University of Texas. He did not believe it, but later changed his mind. In fact, he eventually concluded that many freshmen at Southwest Texas were receiving better instruction in English than he had as a freshman at the state university. The same was probably true in the history and science departments. His reasons for reaching these conclusions were that most instructors of freshmen at the state university were either graduate students or senior professors teaching classes of three and four hundred. Derrick felt that teachers at Southwest Texas made up for their lack of advanced degrees with teaching experience and dedication. In addition, there was the matter of personal contact. Many students became personal friends with their professors. There were frequent opportunities, moreover, for consultation outside of class.[15]

Former students and faculty members who were on the campus in the 1920's often remark that there were many fine teachers at the college. They usually mention M. L. Arnold in history; Gates Thomas, Sue Taylor, and L. N. Wright in English; H. M. Greene in government; O. W. Strahan in physical education; E. O. Wiley in education; J. R. Buckner in modern languages; and C. L. Key in chemistry. Many mention also two administrative employees, Bryan Wildenthal, late president of Sul Ross State College, and Tom Nichols, now a professor of business administration at Southwest Texas. Concerning Retta Murphy, numerous former students who attended several other colleges have remarked, "She was the best history teacher I ever had." Most students felt that the strong departments of the college were mathematics, chemistry, biology, history, and education.

The social life of the students was not much like the stereotyped conception of American colleges during the 1920's. Southwest Texas was no "rah rah" school. Girls outnumbered boys three to one. The girls could have three dates a week; curfew was at midnight on weekends and 10:30 on weekdays. A lively date might involve an evening stroll through the fish hatchery or playing bridge. More serious couples might spend the evening spooning on the benches under the live oak trees on the campus quadrangle.

---

[15]Interview with Leland E. Derrick, San Marcos, January 18, 1965.

Few students had cars, and it was against college rules for girls to ride with boys. The girls held periodic parties and dinners in their dormitories at which there were dancing and games. Afterward, they often hiked with their escorts to Williams Drug Store downtown for refreshments. Then students would go to the Palace Theater for one of the latest silent films, such as Red Grange in "One Minute to Play" or Bebe Daniels in "The Campus Flirt." Sometimes at night groups of serenaders would play music beneath the windows of the girls' dormitories after curfew. One writer for the *College Star*, obviously a girl, remarked that the soft notes of the saxophone drifting in through the windows where the girls were studying brought homesick thoughts—sad but sweet, "like a goodnight kiss."[16]

The girls dresssed rather stylishly, perhaps more so than their feminine counterparts on the campuses of the 1950's and 1960's. They wore the short, low-waisted, straight-lined dresses of the 1920's. Their hair was bobbed severely, a style which gave rise to a campus joke about a young man who told his barber not to trim his hair short because he did not want to look effeminate. Girls habitually wore hose and heels on campus, something virtually unheard of today.

The guardian angel of female virtue on the campus was Mary Brogdon, Dean of Women. Clyde Nail once had a job as boiler tender in a girls' dormitory. One night two girls stayed out past curfew and could not get in the front door. They came around to the boiler room to get Nail to let them in. He had a key to open the back door in case of fire; but when he used it, he found Dean Brogdon standing in front of him and "looking as big as a house."[17]

Miss Brogdon became concerned in 1927 about the alarming shortness of co-eds' skirts. The new styles were quite daring; and bare feminine knees were proving a distraction to all males in the classrooms, even the professors. True to the traditions of college administrators, Miss Brogdon called a conference to discuss the problem and accept her solution. Present were the student council, several football heroes who had been coached to say they did not like short skirts, and a fashion "expert." Every-

---

[16]*College Star,* February 2, 1927, p. 3.

[17]Interview with Clyde Nail, San Antonio, December 18, 1964.

one agreed that skirts should be long enough to cover the knees, and an edict to this effect was announced by the dean at an assembly of all girls. The *College Star* reported that most girls let out their hems cheerfully, but a writer using the pen name of Audacious Jones took the good dean to task in a satirical account of the famous meeting on skirts:

"Now, Mr. Birdeye," inquired the Dean cajolingly, "don't you feel that my girls' skirts are, some of them, immodestly short?"
Replied Mr. Birdeye, "As to most boys' opinions, I am unable to say, but as to mine, it depends entirely upon size and conformation of the member and its angle of incidence with the earth's surface."

Audacious claimed that, despite reports to the contrary, many of the more "obvious and brazen flappers" of the college revolted at having to lengthen their skirts.[18]

A place dear to the hearts of all students and faculty at Southwest Texas was "Riverside." The college had acquired a strip of the San Marcos River only a few hundred yards from the campus and had made it into a beautiful swimming and recreation area. There were large trees, grassy slopes, picnic tables, an island with a dancing area and a bandstand, a bath house, and, above all, the limpid San Marcos River. The river had its headwaters only a quarter of a mile upstream where millions of gallons of water bubbled up from the ground. The water was crystal clear and remained about 70° throughout the year. In winter, when the early morning air was much cooler than the river, a cloud of mist rose from the water and often drifted eerily beneath the great cypress trees of the fish hatchery toward the base of the hill where the college stands. In the long, hot summers of South Texas, summers that sometimes last five months, the river was a great attraction. There is an old saying in San Marcos that "once you have been in the river you will be cool the rest of the day."

Riverside was no small part of the attraction of Southwest Texas to summer students. During the summer session the enrollment of the college doubled, mostly from the influx of large numbers of teachers finishing their training. Summer classes began at 7:00 A.M. and were over by noon. In the afternoons, everyone, includ-

---

[18]*College Star*, February 23, 1927, p. 2.

ing faculty, adjourned to the river to keep cool. Each summer Riverside was the scene of the event known as "The Bathing Regatta and Red Cross Life Saving Annual Review," for which all campus organizations made elaborate floats, decorated them with bathing beauties, and floated them down the river past thousands of spectators. The River Parade was preceded by a thrilling event in which more than a thousand Southwest Texas students, clad in "modern" bathing suits, plunged as one into the chill waters upon a signal from the Regatta director, mathematics professor S. M. Sewell. Then there were life-saving demonstrations by star students; one healthy lass once won the coveted title of "Miss Hercules" by towing twenty other girls in the water.

Riverside was also the place where "College Nights" were held. Welcoming parties for new students were given each summer and fall term. President Evans would usually give a little speech in which he reminded all that college life was not just academics. There was the social side; and since there usually were more than twice as many girls as boys, it was the duty of the boys to date more than one girl. After Evans's remarks there would often be a speech and a few songs from Dean Nolle, whom the *College Star* described as "that notorious tenor." Other faculty members might perform, and then there would be refreshments and games. In later years there was dancing.[19]

Athletics had become a large part of campus life by the late 1920's. Evans had hired Drake University graduate Oscar Strahan as coach when Strahan returned from World War I. Strahan's basketball teams started the 1920's playing on outdoor courts and taking their showers by dipping towels into a barrel of water. But by the end of the 1920's there was a new gymnasium and football stadium, and the Bobcat teams had won several championships in basketball and one in football. The college was also represented by teams in tennis and track.[20] There was much talk on the campus about school spirit and "pep." In 1926 the Bobcat football team was riding high until it played its bitter rivals, the Yellowjackets of Howard Payne College of Brownwood, Texas. It was a close game and the Bobcats played courageously, but

[19]*Ibid.*, September 28, 1927, p. 1.
[20]Interview with Oscar Strahan, San Marcos, December 19, 1964.

they lost. After the game there was a spontaneous assembly of students on the quadrangle to cheer the team even in defeat. The *College Star* commented that never had there been such a feeling of "fraternalism" and added that "traditions are woven of such fabric."[21]

When games were to be played with nearby teams such as St. Edward's University in Austin, it was the custom to charter a train for the whole student body and faculty to travel in one happy, singing, cheering throng to the game. Before a big game one year with St. Mary's University in San Antonio, the *College Star* grew quite sanguine and proclaimed that "there's going to be such a crowd of Bobcat boosters down there that our boys will forget they're away from home." It said that the fans were not going to the game as "seat warmers" but would be there "yelling, whistling, pawing the air, and tearing line-up sheets into confetti." With such encouragement it is small wonder that the Bobcats defeated St. Mary's Rattlesnakes 22-0.[22] Faculty members, who went along as chaperones, often joined in the fun; and after one such weekend the *College Star* remarked that the faculty seemed particularly friendly and fraternal that year.[23]

There was considerable hazing of freshmen on the campus. A favorite form was to force freshmen to make speeches on the quadrangle between classes. Once a freshman from East Texas named Simmons was heard by an upperclassman to criticize certain practices at the college. He was told to get a lard can and stand on it on the quadrangle at a busy time and make a speech on the price of eggs. It developed that Simmons knew much more about the price of eggs than anyone dreamed. He held forth on egg economics for some time, and his curious East Texas drawl and finely developed sense of humor drew a crowd of more than 200 amused students.[24]

No social fraternities or sororities were allowed on the campus, but there were literary societies. The girls had the Shakespeares, the Idyllics, the Philosophians, the Pennybackers, and others. These clubs held regular meetings; and although they

---

[21]*College Star,* October 22, 1926, p. 2.

[22]*Ibid.,* November 2, 1927, p. 1.

[23]*Ibid.,* November 10, 1926, p. 1.

[24]*Ibid.,* November 17, 1926, p. 2.

paid lip service to literary activities, the meetings were largely parties and social gatherings. About once a term they had parties or dances to which they invited their boy friends. There were also boys' literary or debating societies such as the Harris-Blairs and the Jeffersonians. Lyndon Johnson was a Harris-Blair.

The intellectual atmosphere of the college, according to some former students, was "stimulating"; but others say that it suffered by comparison with bigger schools such as the University of Texas. There were student publications such as the *College Star,* the *Pedagog* (the annual), and a student literary review. There were frequent dramatic and literary presentations and performances of musicians and choral groups. Art exhibits were common, as were guest speakers. The speakers included Carl Sandburg, Cornelia Otis Skinner, and Alexander Kerensky; but there were also less impressive ones like Charley Paddock, Olympic champion sprinter, who thrilled his audiences with remarks like "The football team is as strong as its weakest member," and "A country is as strong as its athletes."[25] And then there was W. A. Sutton, superintendent of schools of Atlanta, Georgia, who addressed the students on the subject of "Mouth Hygiene, Health and Education." Sutton blamed most of the ills of the world, including physical abnormality and crime, on improper hygiene. However, the editor of the *College Star* saw the defects in Sutton's theme. He pointed out that tooth decay was not the root of all evil, and he commented that Sutton had become a little overwrought when he concluded that one would be a "traitor to one's progenitors" if he did not brush his teeth faithfully.[26]

The weekly assembly or chapel program was mandatory for all students and was held in the auditorium in the Old Main building. The stage was always occupied by President Evans, Dean Nolle, and Dean of Men Speck. Students claimed to believe that the roof would fall in if those three men were not present. Evans offered the same prayer every time, Nolle made announcements, a program or speaker would usually follow, and then Speck would growl, "Let's get that Bobcat spirit!" The senior class would respond with a yell for the football or basketball

---

[25]*Ibid.,* October 22, 1928, p. 1.
[26]*Ibid.,* November 3, 1928, p. 1.

team. In chapel each class sat in a separate part of the hall, and each student was assigned a seat. Proctors took attendance, and failure to attend would subject a student to disciplinary action.[27]

In summary, it seems fair to say of Southwest Texas State College in the 1920's that it was doing a good job of being what it was supposed to be: a regional college. It was providing higher education, largely at state expense, for the young men and women of South Central Texas. In many cases it was giving such education to students who would never have been able to get it anywhere else because of lack of money. Perhaps its graduates were not as highly polished as those of great univerities; but in terms of what it was doing for its students, Southwest Texas may have been accomplishing comparatively more than the big universities. As Lyndon Johnson said in his letter to Dean Nolle, the college took raw country boys and girls and turned them out as reasonably well-educated men and women ready for productive careers. The proof of this assertion lies in the list of graduates of Southwest Texas. It includes literally thousands of successful teachers, principals, superintendents, and six college presidents. Nearly two hundred graduates have proceeded to doctoral degrees and become professors and research scientists. Several hundred have become doctors and dentists. Thousands have become successful businessmen. Southwest Texas graduates include state senators, United States attorneys, and one President of the United States.

---

[27]Interview with Clyde Nail, San Antonio, December 18, 1964.

V.

A YOUNG MAN IN A HURRY

I

WHY DID LYNDON JOHNSON CHOOSE SOUTHWEST TEXAS AS his college? The University of Texas at Austin was closer and undeniably a good school. Johnson's maternal great-grandfather had been president of Baylor University in Waco, only about a hundred miles away. And there were other schools. Apparently, many reasons prompted Johnson to select the college at San Marcos. It was close, only about thirty miles away; and by all accounts Johnson thought at the time that he wanted to be a teacher, at least for a while. Southwest Texas was a good teachers' college, and its hold on the Hill Country was strong. Nearly everyone who ever went to college from Blanco or Johnson City went there.

Another attraction of Southwest Texas was its small size. It must be remembered that the communities in which Lyndon Johnson grew up were small—numbering only a few hundred people. Most youngsters from such a rural or thinly populated area would be frightened at the thought of going off to school at a huge university with thousands of students and faculty. Southwest Texas was a place where such young people could fit in comfortably. Most of the other students there were from rural areas and small towns. The enrollment was only about 700; the faculty was small and friendly. Ava Johnson, Lyndon's cousin and childhood playmate, came to Southwest Texas about the same time that he did. She has said that "the teachers seemed to understand the country boy and girl." They gave each student the "personal touch," and youngsters did not get an "inferiority complex about being from the country."[1]

As far as can be determined, all of Johnson's grade school and high school teachers were trained at Southwest Texas. It seems warranted to say that, since Johnson never attended any other college, all of his formal education was either at Southwest Texas or by teachers who graduated from the college. In this sense he is uniquely a product of the institution. In 1924, the year Lyndon Johnson graduated from high school, he came with his high school debate team and a teacher to an interscholastic meet on the campus at San Marcos. Quite possibly it was the first college campus he had ever visited.

Another factor in selecting Southwest Texas was that Lyndon Johnson already knew a number of people there. His favorite cousin, Ava, was there. Her mother ran a boarding house for college girls in San Marcos, and several of his friends were in school there. In addition, Sam Johnson was acquainted with the president of the college, C. E. Evans, having met him through his political activities in Austin.

Very likely, however, the strongest attraction at Southwest Texas was that it was an inexpensive school. Johnson had only a hundred dollars with which to go to college, and there would be none

---

[1] Interview with Ava Johnson Cox, Johnson City, August 14, 1964.

after that from home. He had to go to a college where he could earn his way and where the expenses would be low. Southwest Texas was just such a college. Undoubtedly, Rebekah Johnson, in her conversation by telephone with President Evans about Lyndon's coming to Southwest Texas, made arrangements for her son to get a job at the college.

There remains one final consideration in Johnson's choice: he had to validate his high school credits, and Southwest Texas offered him a way to make himself admissable. High schools in Texas were of uneven quality; and in an effort to standardize them, the legislature had provided that to be fully accredited, they would have to affiliate with the state university. Johnson City was not fully affiliated; therefore, not all of its credits were acceptable for entrance at Southwest Texas or any other state institution. Only those credits recognized by the State Board of Education could be used for college entrance. Southwest Texas offered a means, however, by which credit from unaffiliated high schools could be validated. Students could enroll in the sub-college, a laboratory school for all grades, and "prove" those credits on their high school transcript which were in question.[2]

Not many high school graduates understood affiliation; and many came to Southwest Texas expecting to be admitted, only to be told that they would have to prove some of their credits. The unpleasant chore of explaining this situation to students belonged to David Votaw, an education professor. Votaw had endured many disagreeable experiences in telling students they would have to return to high school for a while before they could enter college. Some of them became angry and stormed out of the office; others tried to persuade him to change his decision; some girls wept. Many, knowing that their credits were in doubt, approached the conference with fear and uncertainty.

In the hundreds of times that Votaw held these interviews, there were two students who impressed him by the way they took the news in a positive manner, did not react emotionally, and only inquired what needed to be done. One was a tall, thin, rather handsome young man from Johnson City. According to Votaw, Lyndon Johnson had planned a program for himself,

---

[2]Interview with E. O. Wiley, San Marcos, December 16, 1964.

understood what needed to be done, and was perfectly willing to go into the sub-college to prove some of his credits. The two sat and chatted pleasantly for half an hour. Votaw was impressed by the young man—he had his future all planned; he knew where he was going.[3]

Thus, Lyndon Johnson enrolled in the Southwest Texas sub-college on February 8, 1927. He had only a few credits to prove, one of them in English; and proving them was simply a matter of establishing his proficiency in the subjects. In six weeks, a much shorter time than usual, he had satisfied his teachers and was admitted to the college. Technically speaking, he had graduated from high school in the Southwest Texas sub-college. He enrolled in college for the spring quarter on March 21, 1927. Except for nine months while he taught at Cotulla, Texas, he attended the college continuously, including summers, until August, 1930, when he graduated with a baccalaureate degree with a major in history. He also took the necessary hours in education to obtain a permanent secondary teaching certificate. Johnson spent eleven quarters in resident instruction; in addition, he completed the equivalent of a quarter's work in extension courses while he was teaching at Cotulla. The pattern which he followed was not unusual at Southwest Texas; in fact, many students absolved the requirements for the degree in this way.

Lyndon Johnson earned a creditable academic record in college, and his grades in the social sciences were excellent. In these fields—of particular interest to a man who would one day be president—he completed the following courses: the survey courses in American history; a diplomatic history of the United States; Texas history; numerous courses in advanced American history, especially diplomatic; two very interesting courses under Professor H. M. Greene titled "Problems of Organization and Control of the National Government"; local government; comparative government; community service; the introductory courses in economics and sociology; and courses in "Community Activities on the Rural Level," and "Race Relations."

Johnson's teachers at Southwest Texas who are still on the faculty were R. A. Tampke and Tom Nichols. Others were O. W. Strahan, E. O. Wiley, W. R. Boucher, H. E. Speck, Grace Mc-

---

[3]Interview with David Votaw, San Marcos, June 11, 1964.

Clain, H. M. Greene, J. C. Jones, E. W. Bowman, E. Jones, H. T. Donaho, Bryan Wildenthal, L. N. Wright, Henry Shands, M. L. Arnold, Gates Thomas, W. I. Woodson, Dora Netterville, C. E. Chamberlin, and S. M. Sewell.

The teacher who had the greatest influence on young Lyndon was H. M. Greene, professor of government, who was something of an institution at Southwest Texas. He was a rugged individualist in the academic community. He liked to put college presidents and deans in their proper places. He harassed and heckled administrators and played the role of a nonconforming academic maverick. Refusing to follow the acceptable pattern of professorial behavior, he acted as he pleased both on and off the campus. In short, he was a thorn in the side of his superiors; and the students loved him for his recalcitrance. The spirit of the American West flowed in Greene's veins. Like Henry David Thoreau and the Rocky Mountain Fur Trappers, he loved and needed the solitude and beauty of the wilderness. His "Walden Pond" was a deep, clear spring in a ravine bounded by the rugged hills known as the Devil's Backbone in the Hill Country west of San Marcos. It was one of the most beautiful spots in Texas. Beside the spring, Greene had built a cabin. It was shaded by great live oaks, Spanish oaks, and elms. Deer came to drink at the spring, and wild turkeys flew down the ravine at dusk. Occasionally, the buzz of a rattlesnake disturbed the tranquility of a spring evening. The little hollow remains today virtually unspoiled by human hands. There is not a house within miles of it.

It was at his Hill Country retreat that Greene read, meditated, and escaped the problems of the world. He loved the scenery and animals of the rough Texas hills. A true conservationist, he never killed, fished, or disturbed the trees and grass. Greene's outdoor qualities were reflected in his personal appearance. As a young man he had been very handsome and well dressed, but as he grew older he cared less and less about looking like a professor. He appeared often for class in a faded khaki shirt and worn trousers; once, in the depths of the depression, he was mistaken for a tenant farmer in need of employment. All of this mattered little to Professor Greene. He loved teaching and he loved students, and the students responded in kind.

Professor H. M. Greene

Politically, Greene was somewhere in the gray area between liberalism and radicalism. His liberalism was of the Jeffersonian type, a belief in the democratic processes and protection of individual liberties; in his radicalism, he was something of a Populist—one who advocated control of the big vested interests and assumption of more social and economic responsibility by a stronger national government.

Perhaps Greene's most engaging quality was his arrogant self-confidence. This can be best illustrated by something that happened in the 1940's. It was during the war and a new president, Dr. John G. Flowers, had come to the college. Enrollment was down, and Flowers decided that it would be a good time for members of the faculty who had not acquired their doctoral degrees to go off to graduate school. He announced this policy in faculty meeting, and some teachers enrolled in universities immediately; however, Greene made no effort to comply. He held a master's degree from the University of Texas and had completed a year's work toward a doctorate at the University of Illinois, but that was in 1923. When Flowers called Greene into his office to talk over the matter, Greene told him there was no graduate school that he could attend. Flowers did not understand this remark, and it was several minutes before it dawned on him that Greene was saying there were no graduate professors who could teach him anything.[4]

It might well be that Greene would have wasted his time going back to graduate school. Although well-read, he was not a scholarly man; one of his colleagues said of him that he seemed to absorb ideas by osmosis. He read newspapers and magazines voraciously, and he was skillful at "picking" the minds of others in reading and conversation. Greene was an original thinker. He had his own ideas about history and government, and they did not come out of other men's books.

In class he followed the Socratic method; that is, he headed the discussion of students toward certain conclusions, making them think they had reached them themselves. In his own words: "Often there were small groups of boys in a class, all *interested* in government and politics. On those occasions classes were conducted as a 'seminar.' I posed the issues and they discussed and debated them under my guidance." These discussions sometimes became quite heated, and Greene remembers that the two most ardent antagonists were Lyndon Johnson, who took the more

[4]Interview with John G. Flowers, San Marcos, December 18, 1964.

liberal view, and a boy from one of the old families of San Marcos named Henry Kyle, who was by nature conservative. According to Greene, "I *never* saw Lyndon 'outdone' by a student, though Henry Kyle often *pushed* him to his [Lyndon's] best."[5]

In the class with Lyndon Johnson and Henry Kyle sat a very perceptive young woman named Birdie King. She is now editor of the *Texas Federation News,* a quarterly publication of the Texas Federation of the Blind. Of the class she says, "I have felt the impact of that course on my life more deeply than any other." She maintained that every gifted teacher, once in his career, had one particular class which brought into focus his genius. She was positive that for Professor Greene it was the class she was in. She remembered that Greene "hammered home the responsibilities of the private citizen and the public servant," and that he would criticize and point out defects of a democracy and yet leave his students with the conviction that democracy was worth any price to freedom-loving people. She also remembered Lyndon Johnson well. It was thought that he was headed for a career in politics; and on several occasions, according to Miss King, Greene would turn to Johnson and say, "Son, if I were headed for the political arena, I would bear in mind that the United States Senate is one spot where a man of integrity has a real opportunity to serve his country."[6]

Greene has confirmed that he encouraged Lyndon to pursue a career of poltics. Of Johnson, he says:

I did not expect Lyndon to choose a career in teaching— though I felt and still feel he had been a success at Cotulla. My "encouragement" was toward politics. Clearly, there his *superior* talents lay. I never saw them beat. He was clearly the best student in government and politics I ever had the pleasure of teaching.

Johnson was not the only student that Greene pushed toward a career in politics; "there were several others; Lyndon was just the most successful one!"[7] It is impossible to assess how much of Greene's political philosophy Lyndon Johnson absorbed, but it is obvious that Greene had a profound effect upon him. For in-

---

[5]H. M. Greene to E. C., September 16, 1964.
[6]San Marcos *Record,* January 23, 1964, p. 6.
[7]H. M. Greene to E. C., September 16, 1964.

stance, many similarities can be seen in Johnson's philosophy of the political consensus and the following statement which Greene made often and which was quoted by Willard Deason, another student of the late 1920's: "Democracy is of necessity a compromise. It is made of strongminded men who cannot all prevail as individuals. Therefore, their concerted action must be a compromise."[8]

Professor Greene retired in 1957 to a little cabin deep in the Ozark Mountains of Missouri. He has kept in touch with his star student; and when that student was inaugurated president of the United States, Greene occupied a place of honor. Today he is a frequent guest at the White House, and very likely is still teaching lessons in history and government.

When Lyndon Johnson came to Southwest Texas, he was a friendly, aggressive, clean-cut young man, so striking in his appearance that he often attracted the attention of strangers. A former girl friend described him as "very handsome—tall, thin, with dark, curly hair." She said also that he was very ambitious and had an "overwhelming" personality, and that his feeling toward politics was like that of a "child fascinated by a circus." Those who knew him while he was a student cannot agree on whether he planned a career in politics or in teaching. Those who are probably closest to the truth say that he planned to use teaching as a stepping stone to a career in politics if he could.

A remark made of Johnson by nearly everyone who knew him is that "we knew he was going somewhere." He was obviously a young man in a hurry. One man who worked with him said, "It pained him to loaf." Others remember seeing him walking with his great strides up the hill to the college with his nose buried in a book. He believed in wasting neither time nor effort. He gave up baseball because there was too little return for the energy invested. A literature course in novels was difficult for him because he had no patience with fiction; he was interested only in books that were true.

He was much more mature than most other students. As one of his close friends put it, "He was way ahead of the rest of us. He went to the Democratic Convention in Houston, and the rest

---

[8]Interview with Willard Deason, Austin, December 17, 1964.

of us didn't even know they were having one."[9] His fascination with politics was so great that most of his fellow-students expected him to hold office some day. Some say they thought he would be governor. Once, in the early 1930's, a Southwest Texas student and a University of Texas student toured Europe together. The boy from San Marcos spent hours telling his companion about a fellow at his school named Johnson who was so brilliant and had such drive and knowledge of politics that he might even be president some day.[10]

By all accounts, Johnson was an extremely likeable young man who had a warm greeting for everyone. His manners toward older people were flawless. He had the knack of calling attention to himself, of making a good impression, without being obvious. Despite his constant hurry and involvement in countless activities, he had time to talk with everyone from President Evans to Cayetano Mendez, the janitor of Old Main building. In fact, he became a close friend of both men. Today, Cayetano, long since retired, sits in the front room of his simple frame house in the Southside or Latin part of San Marcos and tells visitors in broken English and with a deep chuckle, "Good friend of mine, still, now—the President of the United States."[11]

Wilton Woods, a classmate and close friend, remembers that once on a trip he and Johnson stopped at a roadside cafe and got a bowl of chili, a favorite dish in Texas. After they finished, Johnson went up to the woman who ran the cafe, shook her hand, and said that it was the finest bowl of chili he had ever eaten. Woods says the chili was not that good.[12]

Most of Johnson's schoolmates agree that he was something of a ladies' man. He did not have a date every night because he did not have the money and there were many other things to be done; but he dated many girls, usually two or three nights a week. His first roommate, Barton Gill, recalls that Johnson was a neat dresser on a very limited wardrobe. His trademark was a bow tie. Gill remembers many times seeing Johnson stand before

[9]Interview with Wilton Woods, Seguin, December 22, 1964.
[10]Interview with W. Eugene Hollon, Norman, Oklahoma, December 27, 1964.
[11]Interview with Cayetano Mendez, San Marcos, December 11, 1964.
[12]Interview with Wilton Woods, Seguin, December 22, 1964.

a mirror smoothing down his curly hair, "drawing his neck down into his collar so that it would not look so long, and carrying on a lively banter with Gill about how irresistible they were to girls."[13]

Apparently Johnson had little time for the petty vices which most college boys indulge in, and yet he was certainly "one of the boys." He was a non-drinker except for an occasional beer. When his cronies spent all night playing poker, he had other things to do. But if there was a "bull session," especially one on politics, he would stay as long as anyone else was there. No one ever remembered his saying, "I'm tired; I'm going to bed."

Johnson had a close circle of friends. He was intensely loyal to them; and although he was always friendly to other boys, one who admired him greatly found him "evasive" and hard to get to know.[14] Once Johnson and a group of his close friends were sitting around a boarding house wishing they could go to Mexico for the weekend. One boy had a Ford car, but no one had enough money to buy gasoline. Johnson thought about it for a while and then turned to Vernon Whitesides and asked, "Where is that Real Silk sample case?" Real Silk was the brand name for a line of hosiery sold only by door-to-door salesmen. Whitesides was agent for the company, and Johnson sold for him. Whitesides got the case and Johnson left with it. Three hours later he returned; he had sold enough hose to make twenty dollars profit. His first customer had been President Evans. The twenty dollars paid for a weekend for four boys in the border town of Nuevo Laredo.[15]

Johnson never missed an opportunity to go to Austin to watch the state legislature when it was in session. He went to hear the speeches, but he especially wanted to hear Governor Jim Ferguson when he spoke. Johnson was always full of ideas on politics and ready to work in any campaign.[16] According to one of the inner circle of friends, "Lyndon was brilliant; he had a high I.Q., but he always wanted to be the head man. He kept his eye

---

[13]Interview with Barton Gill, San Marcos, December 20, 1964.

[14]Interview with Clyde Nail, San Antonio, December 18, 1964.

[15]Interview with Willard Deason, Austin, December 17, 1964.

[16]Interview with Fenner Roth, Corpus Christi, March 6, 1965.

on what he wanted. Every action was calculated to advance his career. He left no stone unturned."[17]

He had little money while he was in college, but he was not appreciably poorer than most of his friends, many of whom lived entirely on their earnings from the college. Johnson once developed a toothache and had no money to pay for a dentist, but he had an uncle in San Antonio who would do the work free. With Willard Deason for company, Lyndon hitchhiked the fifty miles to San Antonio to get the filling.[18] His first job at Southwest Texas was on the clean-up crew which picked up papers, rocks, and trash. He soon went to the office of the president, applied to Evans for a better job, and was made assistant to Leandro Gonzales, janitor in the Science Building. Legend has it that Johnson would practice debating and political speaking while pushing a big broom down the deserted halls of the Science Building late at night, but none of the janitors remember hearing him do it.[19]

He continued to apply to Evans for better jobs, and finally Evans found one for him as special assistant to the secretary in the president's office. This was quite an honor; no student had ever held the job before. The president's secretary was Tom Nichols, and soon Johnson occupied a desk next to him. People who entered the office got the impression that Lyndon Johnson was running things, and rumors circulated that visitors had to get Johnson's permission to see the president. Since there were no inter-departmental telephones on the campus, one of Johnson's primary duties was to carry messages from the college president to various departments. In this capacity he became well-known to key faculty members and was looked upon as a representative of the administration.[20]

The relationship between Lyndon Johnson and President C. E. Evans played a very important part in the development of the future politician. Evans recognized early the tremendous potential of Sam Johnson's son, and took him under his wing to tutor him in politics. He took Johnson to Austin with him

[17]Interview with Horace Richards, Corpus Christi, March 4, 1965.
[18]Interview with Willard Deason, Austin, December 17, 1964.
[19]Interview with Antonio Aranda, San Marcos, December 11, 1964.
[20]Interview with Tom Nichols, San Marcos, March 31, 1965.

when he had to appear before legislative committees or when he wished to hear debates. He had Johnson prepare many of his letters to politicians and reports to state agencies, and in the process he taught him what he knew about state problems.[21] For his part, Johnson greatly admired Evans. A campus legend has it that Lyndon Johnson was the first student to slap President Evans on the back. Johnson knew instinctively when he first came to the campus where the power was—in the president. One day he was walking across the campus with his cousin Ava Johnson. She was carrying her copy of the *Pedagog* in which one of her favorite professors had written for her, "Keep your mind open. There is lots to be learned that is not written in books." In her own words, Ava was "just a little country girl" who believed that all she had to do to get ahead in college was to keep her nose in books. Ava told Lyndon of the professor's advice, and he said: "Ava, that is the best thing that was ever written for you. The first thing you want to do is to know people . . . and don't play sandlot ball; play in the big leagues . . . get to know the first team." Ava knew that Lyndon had done exactly that with President Evans, but she was aghast at the idea of doing it herself. "Why, Lyndon," she said, "I wouldn't dare to go up to President Evans's office!" He replied, "That's where you want to start."[22]

2

When Johnson was a student at Southwest Texas, he lived in a number of boarding houses: one on North Austin Street, another on West Hopkins, and still another on North Comanche. He took his meals on Edward Gary Street at the boarding house of Mrs. Gates, a plump, motherly woman, of whom he became quite fond. In later years, when he returned to the campus, he always greeted her with a big embrace. Mrs. Gates had a special rule at her table: boarders could eat all they wanted, but when they reached for the meat they had to keep one foot on the floor. Johnson, with his long arms, developed a formidable boarding house reach. He loved pork chops, and Mrs. Gates cooked only one chop per boarder; but when one of the regulars was late to

---

[21]Interview with Ethel Davis, San Marcos, December 14, 1964.

[22]Interview with Ava Johnson Cox, Johnson City, August 14, 1964.

the table, Johnson's fork could be expected to come sailing down the length of the table with unerring aim to spear the missing boy's pork chop.[23]

After he became assistant secretary to President Evans, Johnson and a friend named Alfred Johnson moved into a room above the president's garage. Alfred Johnson, nicknamed "Booty," was a star football player and a close friend of Lyndon's. The two were not related, although many people thought they were. Called "Johnson and Johnson" on the campus, they had met when both were working on the clean-up crew; and later, when Lyndon began working in the president's office, he got a job for Booty as "inspector of buildings."

Contrary to many reports, the room above Evans's garage was decently furnished; but since it did not have a shower, the boys did their bathing at the men's gymnasium across the street until the coach caught them and reported them to the business manager. The two Johnsons could not always pay their rent, and Evans allowed them to work it out by painting the garage. One spring they painted the garage three times.[24]

Another important phase of Lyndon Johnson's development at Southwest Texas was his participation on the college debate team. Debate in those days was taken seriously, the *College Star* reporting the engagements of the debate team with almost as much fanfare as it did those of the football team. John G. Flowers, who was president of the college from 1942 to 1964, recalled that when he was a student at the college before World War I, a successful debate team which returned after a victorious encounter with a rival school was once met at the railroad station by the entire student body and pulled up the hill to the college in a buggy by a team of ten boys.[25]

The debate coach was Professor Greene, and his star debaters were Lyndon Johnson and Elmer Graham. The three made a good team; they won most of their debates. Greene was completely inept at organizing materials in preparation for the debates and in planning strategy, but he was a master at finding off-beat items that the opposition had never heard of. In college

[23]Interview with Clyde Nail, San Antonio, December 18, 1964.
[24]Interview with Alfred Nolle, San Marcos, June 11, 1964.
[25]Interview with John G. Flowers, San Marcos, December 14, 1964.

debate it is necessary for a team to prepare to take either side of the question, and the debaters may not know whether they are the affirmative or the negative until immediately before the debate begins. In later years Lyndon Johnson wrote Elmer Graham that this training in seeing both sides had helped him do the same thing in his public career.

It was Graham's job on the team to lay out the facts in a logical manner; Johnson did not relish this task. Then the strategy called for Johnson to pick up a point which the opposition had made and tear it to pieces. Hopefully, this would leave the impression that the same thing could be done to any of the other points made by the opposition. According to Graham, Johnson was particularly effective at hammering away at the weakness of the opponents. When he got them down, he was ruthless in not letting them find a way to recover. He never got angry at the other team, however, and never took the arguments personally. Nor did he complain about the decision of the judges. Graham says Johnson was good at reacting to new arguments and at thinking on his feet, but that he did not have a particularly wide knowledge of world affairs. Johnson worked hard at familiarizing himself with the specific issues to be debated, however, and became an expert on them.

The team traveled all over the state to debate with other colleges, and Graham was impressed by the fact that wherever Lyndon Johnson went he was never a stranger long. He introduced himself in every group he entered and made friends with amazing speed. Graham, who later became a Baptist minister and was doing some preaching even during his student days, was a very moral, perhaps straight-laced young man. Traveling with Professor Greene and Lyndon Johnson, he was occasionally shocked. Greene, he thought, was capable of being quite crude; and Johnson bothered him occasionally with a bad word, but he liked and admired both of them.[26]

3

Lyndon Johnson's involvement in another phase of college life should be recorded in considerable detail because it fore-

---

[26]Interview with Elmer Graham, San Antonio, December 18, 1964.

shadows the development of his later career. His participation in campus politics gives evidence, even at this early age, of his talent for organizing and leading others to attain the goals that he set. His interest in politics grew accordingly as he found at Southwest Texas the first opportunity to practice the skill that was to become the dominant force in his life.

Southwest Texas State was a small college with a great sameness about its students, although deep cross currents existed in its social and political life. One of these was the resentment against football players and athletes felt by boys who were not athletes. On the campus in the late 1920's this feeling was particularly strong because of the new success of athletics at the college. During his first ten years as football coach, Oscar Strahan had developed some fine teams, and the football heroes became numerous on the campus. The old song of that era about how "you've got to be a football hero to get along with the beautiful girls" was true at Southwest Texas. In addition, the football players enjoyed other advantages: they went to the head of the line at the cafeteria; they got preference in housing; they were allowed to register first during enrollment; and, although all other students were required to attend chapel faithfully, the football players could cut without fear of punishment.[27]

The football players were the social lions of the campus. The great social event of the year was the banquet and dance given in their honor each winter by the Shakespeare Literary Society. The Shakespeares were considered, at least by themselves, to be the leading social club on the hill and to have the prettiest girls as members. The club was made up mostly of "town" girls from San Marcos who were more than a little snobbish. Their annual banquet took two weeks to prepare, and some of the students complained that everything on the campus stopped while the preparations were being made. In addition to the Shakespeares and the varsity football players, the banquet was attended by President Evans, the deans of the college, and the coaches. There were speeches and awards, and it was the custom for the football team to elect the captains for the next season. It was a glorious

[27]Interview with Clyde Nail, San Antonio, December 18, 1964.

evening for those who attended, but about ninety per cent of the student body was not invited.[28]

In campus politics the football players were also supreme. Student politics in those days at Southwest Texas had real meaning. Each class elected a slate of officers, including a president, vice-president, student council representative, and yell leader. Student council representative was a key post because the council decided how the student activity fee would be spent. This tax was a levy placed on each student in order to pay for his admission to college athletic contests and entertainments. The fee also supported the *College Star* and Riverside Park. It was the student council that elected the editors of the *Star* and the *Pedagog* and the business manager of the *Pedagog*. These jobs were highly prized because they paid a salary of thirty dollars per month, enough to support a student in school.

Since the mid-1920's, the student council and the staffs of the *Star* and *Pedagog* had been dominated by the football players. They had achieved their political power through an organization known on the campus as the Black Stars. In reality the name was Beta Sigma; but that, like the membership of the club, was a secret. Some students who were not members learned that the initials of the name were "B.S."; since the emblem of the college was a star, they assumed that "B.S." stood for Black Stars. Made up altogether of athletes, the Black Stars began largely as a social organization which held frequent picnics and parties with their girl friends. Coach Strahan and his wife attended these functions, and Strahan was often referred to on the campus as "the Black Star." In its operation the organization was much like a college Greek-letter social fraternity. Any member could nominate a new member, but a unanimous vote was necessary for approval. The club was first organized in 1920, and for years all varsity football players were taken into membership automatically. But in the late 1920's membership became more and more exclusive, and not all football players were invited to join. In the early 1920's Coach Strahan recognized that the club was causing dissension on the football squad and withdrew his support. He even attempted to kill the organization, but it continued to operate in secret through the mid-1930's.

[28]Interview with Oscar Strahan, San Marcos, December 19, 1964.

In campus politics the Black Stars ran candidates for every office and usually won. There was no organized opposition, and the votes of the athletes plus those of other students they were able to influence, especially girls, were usually enough to win. Some of the students on the campus felt, however, that the Black Stars were arrogant and intolerable. According to one, "They looked down their noses at the rest of us." Although the membership of the Black Stars was secret, most students knew that nearly all football players were members. Campus leaders like Henry Shands, Ed Kallina, Jesse Kellam, and Alfred Johnson were generally recognized as Black Stars.[29]

It was natural that a rival organization of non-athletes would eventually spring up. Its actual origins are a bit obscure, since it was highly secret at the time; and the memories of the members after thirty-five years are somewhat hazy. Apparently, the organization known as the White Stars was founded in the fall of 1928 at a meeting of six or seven boys, including Lyndon Johnson, Vernon Whitesides, Horace Richards, Willard Deason, Wilton Woods, Hollis Frazer, and perhaps several others. One account of the founding of the White Stars comes from Alfred Johnson, Lyndon's roommate. According to his recollection, he encouraged Lyndon to go out for baseball so that he would be eligible for membership in the Black Stars. But Lyndon did not have enough time to devote to the sport; thereupon, Alfred decided to try to get him into the club anyway, since Lyndon worked in the president's office and "could help us out if we needed it." Alfred Johnson says, however, that when the vote was taken among the members, there was one black ball. He thought it came from a boy who was "mad because Lyndon had been courting his girl." According to Alfred, Lyndon "didn't get sore about it, but he went right out and organized a rival group popularly called the White Stars."[30]

None of the original White Stars remembers Alfred Johnson's story, and no one recalls exactly who originated the club. Most say that it was organized by several boys, among them Lyndon

---

[29]Interview with Oscar Strahan, San Marcos, December 19, 1964.

[30]*The Washington Daily News,* December 26, 1963, p. 20.

[31]Interview with Fenner Roth, Corpus Christi, March 6, 1965.

Johnson. One member taken in later that year stated that he assumed at the time that the club was "Lyndon's brainchild."[31] From the beginning, the purpose of the White Stars was to wrest campus political control from the Black Stars and "to get a place in the sun." The club was to be quite similar to the Black Stars in its organization. It was to be a secret society with a secret name—Alpha and Omega. New members were to be chosen by nomination, and to be approved, a candidate had to be accepted unanimously. Unlike college Greek-letter fraternities which choose new members on the basis of their appearance, dress, grades, money, and family, the White Stars chose their members very carefully from among those boys on the campus who appeared to have the most promise, those who would "do something," and who seemed to have intelligence and ability.[32] After the club was formed, new members were numbered successively as they were inducted. Among the originals there were frequently friendly quarrels about who was number one, but the question was never settled.

The original White Stars were an interesting lot. In addition to the ambitious, gregarious, and tremendously energetic Lyndon Johnson, there was a close friend, Willard Deason. A few years older than Johnson, Deason came from Stockdale, Texas. He met Johnson when they were in a freshman mathematics class together, where the two sat across the aisle from each other. One day in class Deason made a remark which Johnson overheard and said, "Aw, you're crazy as hell!" Deason, who has a fiery temper, seethed through the rest of the class. When it was over he stalked into the hall; but Johnson singled him out, put a friendly arm over his shoulder, and said, "Partner, it's all part of going to college." Their lifelong friendship began there.

Deason was interested in campus politics. As a boy, he had played a game with his father of learning all the county seats of Texas. They also knew every small town in Central Texas. Deason had a phenomenal memory for names. Also, when he met someone for the first time, he made a point of remembering what town that person was from, a difficult feat since most

---

[32]Information on the White Stars comes from interviews with most of the original members. The story has been pieced together from the consensus of these interviews.

of the students at the college were from the small towns of Central Texas. The next time Deason met his new acquaintance, he would ask how things were in the home town. It was a surprise and pleasure to a youngster to have someone remember both his name and his home town. Deason found a very effective device to make friends and become well known on the campus.[33]

Another original White Star was Horace Richards, who claims to have written the first constitution and bylaws of the club and to have sworn in the first members in a mystical ceremony held at night on the banks of the San Marcos River with a burning candle and a Bible. Richards was the campus promoter, whose mind was always turning over ways to make money. Once, during a heated pep rally before the big football game with North Texas State Teachers College, he stood outside trying to think of some way in which he could capitalize on the tremendous emotions being stirred up inside. Finally he got an idea; as the excited students and faculty poured out of the building, he stood by the door with his hat in his hand and yelled, "Kick in for the decorations." He did not say what decorations, but everyone dropped something in his hat. He literally made a hatful of money. Often, before football games, Richards had labels printed which read, "Beat ------" (whoever the opponent was). He would call a meeting of co-eds and sell them dozens of the labels at ten cents each. The girls would then sell them at the same price to boys on the campus and pin them on as part of the bargain. No one seemed to realize that all the profits were going to Richards. Richards and Lyndon Johnson sat together in one class in which the professor seemed to have a fixation on the Hottentots. Every time the professor wanted to illustrate a point he would manage to work them in. Johnson would lean toward Richards and say, "Here come the Hottentots again." Try as he would, Richards could not control himself; he burst out laughing and giggled so much in class that the professor became suspicious and probably gave Richards a lower grade in the course because of his behavior.[34]

Among the original White Stars were Vernon Whitesides and

---

[33]Interview with Willard Deason, Austin, December 17, 1964.
[34]Interview with Horace Richards, Corpus Christi, March 1, 1965.

Wilton Woods. Whitesides was the group's humorist and raconteur, with a keen sense of humor and a strong Texas accent. Woods was from Blanco, Texas. His family had been friends of the Johnson family for years, and Lyndon and Wilton had been boyhood friends. Woods was of very slight build, weighing no more than 120 pounds. He spoke so softly that it was a strain to hear him even at a distance of a few feet. He was probably the most generally liked of the original White Stars.

The White Stars never revealed their true name—Alpha and Omega—but when it became known on the campus that there was a rival group to the Black Stars, many naturally assumed that the name would be White Stars. The mistake was never corrected; in fact, the White Stars thought it was amusing when the wrong name was applied to them. It is significant that the members took vows which even to this day they will not talk about. Obviously there was a vow of secrecy; but there was also probably a pledge of brotherhood, a promise to help each other whenever possible in college and in later life. In this latter regard the organization went beyond its original promise of being strictly a campus political club.

There were only about ten White Stars the first year. The organization had a rule that no more than two of them could be seen together on the campus. If two were joined by a third, they would exchange significant glances and indicate which one was to leave. The club met often, sometimes as frequently as once a week, usually late at night in a student's room. At the meetings the members discussed their strategy in approaching elections, decided who would be their candidates, who would nominate them, who would speak in their behalf, and generally what the parliamentary procedure would be. They counted prospective votes, each member reporting how he thought the students in his house or group would vote. The various voting blocs on the campus were considered—the girls' vote, the YMCA vote, the town vote, the Harris Blair vote, and so on. They speculated as to whom the Black Star candidates would be; and sometimes, when the rival organization had an especially strong candidate, the White Stars devised special strategems. For instance, several times they engineered the nomination to split the opposition vote.

On one occasion, when the White Stars feared defeat in an election for a class presidency, they moved to elect the class officers in reverse order. Then they nominated the most popular Black Star for the relatively unimportant office of cheer leader, and he was elected easily. This left the way clear for them to win the presidency.

One of the fundamental quarrels between the Black Stars and the White Stars was over the student activity fee. When the Black Stars ran the student council, they saw to it that most of the money collected from students in activity fees went for football and other athletic events. The White Stars were determined to gain control of the council in order to redistribute part of the money to activities like the debate team, the college dramatic club, the glee club, special speakers, and music and dramatic programs. Eventually, the White Stars won the fight and the money was appropriated to more cultural and intellectual activities.

As the club grew, the secrecy became more of a problem. In later years it became necessary to remove two members who talked too much about the activities and membership of the club. Since there was no provision in the rules for removal, it was decided simply to quit telling the two when and where the meetings were being held. Some of the White Stars suspected that the two boys involved were Black Star spies who had infiltrated the club.

The White Stars had no officers and no dues. They did not live together in one house but instead were scattered all over town. For example, in his senior year Lyndon Johnson lived in the boarding house of Mrs. Mattie Hopper. His roommate and his "freshman"—every senior had a freshman to run his errands—was Fenner Roth, number thirteen in the White Stars. The other two boys in the house were Elvin Reed and Ardis Hopper (Mrs. Hopper's son), both of whom were Black Stars. Apparently, everyone involved knew the situation, but they were all close friends and there was much banter about it.[35]

Within a year after they were organized, the White Stars became a potent political force on the campus. They elected their members to important offices, they gained control of the stu-

[35]Interview with Fenner Roth, Corpus Christi, March 6, 1965.

dent council, and they became editors of the *College Star* and the *Pedagog*. Lyndon Johnson, as assistant secretary in the president's office, was able to help the White Stars get good student jobs. One student who belonged to neither political group recalls that he could tell when the White Stars gained control because suddenly they had all the inside jobs in offices and the library, and the Black Stars were working outside on the construction and painting crews.[36]

The White Stars were supreme for the next several years. Although there were never more than about thirty active members at any time, they controlled campus politics. They were able to do so by cleverly planning and by organizing students. Many girls and boys enlisted to work actively for the White Star candidates. The club was determined to control the editorial page of the *College Star* and the "Cat's Claw," the humor section of the *Pedagog*, and they were generally able to do so throughout the 1930's, although occasionally the Black Stars won temporary ascendancy in one or the other publications.

The White Stars developed political techniques which would be of great use to them in later life. In class elections it was person-to-person politics. There were no rallies, speeches, signs, or advertisements in the paper. Since there were only about a hundred students in each of the upper classes, every student had to be contacted personally and often had to be convinced by long arguments to vote for the White Star candidates. It is easy to see how such experience helped the naturally gregarious Lyndon Johnson to develop the effective techniques he used later as Senate Majority Leader to sway opinions in a body of voters of about the same size as his senior class.

One example of the political lessons Johnson learned in the White Stars is provided by the election for president of the senior class in the winter term of 1930. The Black Stars had been able to elect a very popular athlete, Dick Spinn, to the office for the previous term; and he was a likely candidate for re-election. The White Stars decided to run Willard Deason, but they knew that Spinn would be difficult to beat. They talked to all the seniors, determined how they planned to vote, and caucused the night

---

[36]Interview with Clyde Nail, San Antonio, December 18, 1964.

« 110 »

before to count the possible votes. Anticipating about ninety ballots, the White Stars estimated that Deason was some fifteen votes behind, seemingly too large a margin to overcome; and most of the boys, feeling that they were beaten, decided to go to bed. But Lyndon Johnson, who was not ready to give up, began telephoning the girls' dormitory, went to the boys' boarding houses, and awakened seniors in an effort to persuade them to change their votes. The next day, when the votes were counted, Deason had won by eight votes.

Campus politics was good experience for a future political leader like Lyndon Baines Johnson. Not only did he learn politics on a person-to-person basis; but, like so many White Stars, he learned parliamentary procedure as a member of the Harris Blair Debating Society, which was sponsored by Professor H. M. Greene. He would divide the club into two groups telling one to take one side of a question and the other to take the other side. Then a resolution would be proposed. Perhaps it had no real practical purpose; but the two sides would battle back and forth, using all the parliamentary tricks they could think of to defeat or pass the resolution.[37]

In their heyday the White Stars, which one of the charter members has described as the "brainchild" of Lyndon Johnson, became a potent political force on the campus. But even more important, the organization was the training ground for a generation of capable and successful men. Many went into business; and some of them, such as Horace Richards, Fenner Roth, and Willard Deason, are now, to use a Texas expression, "well fixed." Several White Stars went into politics or became lawyers, among them were a United States attorney, a state senator, and several highly-placed civil servants. In addition, many became teachers, and some rose to prominent positions in education. At least three became members of the faculty at Southwest Texas State, and one became President of the United States. This record is impressive, particularly when one realizes that the organization never had more than 160 members.

---

[37]Interview with Ernest Morgan, San Marcos, March 7, 1965.

VI.

THE JOURNALIST

LYNDON JOHNSON'S CAREER IN COLLEGE JOURNALISM BEGAN before he was actually admitted to college. While he was validating his high school credits at Southwest Texas State in the spring of 1927, his class in composition was assigned the subject "Is thinking popular?" Two of the essays written by members of the class were so good that they were published in the *College Star*. One of these was put in the regular editorial space and given a by-line—that of Lyndon Johnson.

The style of Johnson's essay was simple and direct. There were a few rough spots and inconsistencies and at least one mistake—dating Socrates in the seventh century; but the arguments were sound, and it was not difficult to see why the essay was chosen for publication. The young essayist used historical examples such as Socrates, Columbus, and Roger Williams to establish the point that while new ideas are seldom popular and often bring misery to the thinker, they are less severely penalized today than formerly. The worst that usually happens to a modern original thinker is "ostracism of a kind, ridicule, sarcasm, and indifference." In contrast, there are examples from history of the price that thinkers have been forced to pay: the cup of hemlock which Socrates drank, the chains and poverty of Columbus, and the trial and expulsion of Williams. "The masses are now," wrote Johnson, "more tolerant of independent thought." He attributed this to tolerance of "principles written into our constitution."

The real reward for thinking, he continued, is not in acclaim of contemporaries, but in the fact that "succeeding ages single out the great thinkers of the past and accord them the respect and admiration justly theirs." Moreover, he remarked that "time brings the reward their contemporaries dared not give"; and having stated this theme, Johnson further elaborated: "the great men are those who dared to think. They live for time and eternity. All honor to their courageous spirits and deathless minds." Johnson concluded: "If we today wish to live, we must think." He admonished his readers to separate themselves from the common herd, to scorn the creeds and dogmas of the times, and to think for themselves. They should be willing to search for the truth; it would be a difficult task calling for great energy, but it would be a rewarding one which would lead into "beautiful and fruitful realms."[1]

This essay was probably the first written by Lyndon Johnson ever published anywhere. He was only eighteen years old and not yet in college, but it reflected a surprising maturity and ability to use words. The fact that it was published in the college newspaper indicated that Johnson's teacher of composition and the editor of the *Star* thought that here, indeed, was an unusual young man.

[1] *College Star,* March 23, 1927, p. 2.

Only three months after he was admitted to the college, Lyndon Johnson's name began to appear on the masthead of the college newspaper. He was listed variously as assistant and associate editor; and his principal job was to write editorials, which he composed almost weekly for the next nine months. While some of these articles were on strictly campus subjects, most were concerned with matters of broad and general interest and comprised a comprehensive statement of the philosophy and moral code of an eighteen-year-old student from Johnson City.

When Johnson came to Southwest Texas, many of his concepts and beliefs were already formulated. Unlike many college freshmen, he possessed considerable knowledge of history and politics. For instance, in the fall and winter quarters of 1927, Johnson wrote editorials in the *College Star* on the United States Constitution and figures in American history which reflected much greater insight than would normally be gained in an introductory course. At that time he had taken only two survey courses in history and one in government.[2]

The first editorial written by Lyndon Johnson as a member of the *Star* staff was one commemorating Father's Day. From it we gain some insight into his early family life. He looked upon fatherhood as a stoic responsibility. When troubles beset the family, the mother could find comfort in "tears and confidences," but not so the father: "he must square his shoulders, resolutely grit his teeth, suppress his emotions, and with renewed courage meet the issue." As Johnson saw it, there was no opportunity for him to "shirk responsibilities and duties: too many were depending on him." To young Johnson, a father was someone who somehow managed to pay all the bills, who built the family home with his "brains and brawn," and who with "his courage and protective spirit repeled the cruel blows of the world." Indeed, he was the "producer, the provider, and the protector."[3]

The following week, Johnson's editorial was titled "A Plea for Courtesy," in which he maintained that in "this swiftly moving, money-mad age" there was not time for the "civilities and courtesies that were exacted in former years." He saw this as a

---

[2]College transcript of Lyndon B. Johnson on file with Office of the Registrar, Southwest Texas State College.

[3]*College Star*, June 27, 1927, p. 2.

distinct loss and wrote, "there is no present-day man that can equal the charm of the courtly manner of our grandfathers; there is no modern air of sophistication that can compare with the demure graciousness of . . . our grandmothers." Realizing the "greatness of this loss," Johnson said that his Southern blood compelled him to present a "humble plea for the vanishing virtue" of courtesy.

He defined courtesy as "an outward expression of inward kindness of thought and unselfishness of purpose," and contended that it grew out of the "desire to please," its basis being the Golden Rule. Courtesy is "an exquisite flowing of human tolerance and interest." And for those who are courteous, there are rewards: teachers can get more work out of their students; doctors with a "sympathetic and kindly manner" usually have the largest practices in town; and merchants with "pleasant speech" always have "hosts of customers."[4]

The Fourth of July, 1927, inspired another editorial on the subject of the heritage of Independence Day. Johnson saw this national holiday in the grand old style that America once observed it. To boys it was "fire crackers and parades," to politicians it was "stump speeches and handshaking," to farm wives it was a "basket dinner and a picnic," and to the old-timers it was "one more get-together and reminiscence." But there was more to the Fourth of July, he continued, than simply celebration. It was a time to pay homage to the founding fathers of the American republic and to their "dauntless courage . . . foresight . . . wisdom . . . and flaming spirit of liberty." Johnson stated that he was "lost in reverent awe," when considering the founding fathers. He maintained that it was difficult for contemporary Americans adequately to appreciate their heritage:

We who have known only the glorious privileges, the wonderful opportunities, the glorious liberty of life in a great republic can never fully understand how priceless is our heritage. Reared as we have been, the oppressions and tyrannies, the sacrifices, and suffering endured by those patriots, cannot be completely understood. We shall never know what they suffered that we might be spared such indignities and oppressions.

Johnson said, however, there was one thing that was clear: each

[4]*Ibid.*, June 29, 1927, p. 2.

American owed to the patriots who won American independence a debt of gratitude. "Ours is the happy duty," he wrote, "of serving the great nation these heroes brought into existence." This duty also consisted of upholding the laws of the nation "born in their love of liberty," of protecting its principles, and of perpetuating its traditions. In these ways, said Johnson, "we may discharge the debt we owe the founders of this great Nation. . . . May we serve her with our noblest and our best!"[5]

When a co-ed found a "considerable amount" of money which someone had lost and placed an announcement on the bulletin board which said she would return the money to the owner if he could identify the amount, Johnson was inspired to compose another editorial in which he wrote that the young lady's "honesty of soul is a possession of greater value than the wealth of kings." He stated that honesty and a clear conscience are great assets. And yet this "priceless virtue" of honesty can belong to everyone.[6]

After this essay came one on "Happiness." Johnson said that everyone had his own idea of happiness: the poor man thought it was wealth, the schoolboy thought it was maturity with its "responsibilities and privileges," and the businessman thought it was retirement. And yet few people actually achieved happiness. Like honesty, however, happiness was within the reach of everyone. It was not found in the form of material blessings, but instead was "a state of mind and heart" and would thrive under any conditions. Johnson's formula for achieving the happy state of mind was simple: "Live honest, upright lives; choose a lifework suited to individual abilities and highest desires; submerge ego in this work; resolve to be happy *now* instead of planning and dreaming of tomorrow's bliss." He urged his readers to grasp happiness now, thereby increasing their usefulness in proportion to their serenity and making life "vital and joyous instead of humdrum and hopeless."[7]

An editorial which he wrote on a campus problem concerned "The College Exchange," a store operated by the college that

[5]*Ibid.*, July 6, 1927, p. 2.
[6]*Ibid.*, July 21, 1927, p. 2.
[7]*Ibid.*, July 27, 1927, p. 2.

sold school supplies and textbooks to students. It was a monopoly, since there were no other bookstores in town. The Exchange hired student help, published financial statements periodically, and turned over all profits to the "T" Association (the varsity lettermen) and to the College YMCA and YWCA. Students complained, however, about its high prices and the absence of other bookstores. Others complained about the service and the quality of supplies found there. Yet Lyndon, in his editorial, strongly defended the Exchange. He said that most other colleges operated exchanges, and he pointed out that the Exchange not only provided valuable services to students and faculty, but that it also allowed the administration "a certain amount of oversight of class aids, notebooks, reference books, and other articles used in the classroom." He maintained that the Exchange was convenient, that its prices were reasonable, that its attendants (all students "struggling for an education") were courteous and efficient, and that its goods were "first rate."[8] Later in his college career, however, when he became a White Star, Johnson fought and helped end the practice of turning over part of Exchange profits to the "T" Association.

At the end of the summer of 1927, Johnson, who had been on the campus only eight months, wrote an editorial in glowing praise of Southwest Texas State College, which he described as "a splendid training school." Each year, he said, large numbers of young men and women earned degrees and left the college to enter professions, frequently teaching, while some went on to graduate study. Graduates of the college, said Johnson, had "a definite plan of life-work, the longing to achieve chosen ideals in life, and the thorough consecration and determination necessary to consummate this purpose." He felt that "the strength and beauty of the vision gained in these halls" was of "inestimable worth."[9]

When the *College Star* resumed publication in the fall, its masthead listed the one and only "editorial writer" as Lyndon B. Johnson. One of his first editorials of the new school year reflected his developing journalistic style. It was titled "Guilty

[8]*Ibid.*, August 10, 1927, p. 2.
[9]*Ibid.*

« 117 »

of a Wasted School Year," and he warned fellow-students that unless they were careful, many of them would waste their time as they had done during the previous year. He cautioned that the opportunities of the coming year would mean nothing unless students were "able to recognize them and . . . able to grasp them." He urged, "Make your plans and begin." He promised that every "cherished ambition" with a "logical foundation" could be accomplished with work, and he concluded that if dreams were worth anything they were worth working for.[10]

In another editorial called "He Who Conquers," the young editor had some revealing observations to make about the greatest hero of the 1920's, Charles Lindberg. He said that Lindberg's great feat of flying the Atlantic was not all luck; much of it was pluck. Lindberg's courage and strength came from within, from self-mastery. Johnson noted that "when self has been conquered, victory over life's temptations and weaknesses comes easily—Lindberg found it so." He admired Lindberg's ability to resist the temptations of success—his disdain of the adulation of the "overzealous," his modesty, his poise, and his democratic spirit. He wrote, "it is a wonderful thing to make the first trans-ocean flight and achieve spiritual independence. Still more wonderful is the fact that this feat lies within the grasp of all of us." This last remark, which was now becoming characteristic of Johnsonian editorials, was followed by another consistent feature of his writing, an exhortation to his fellow students to follow the example: "The choice lies with you. Do not sigh for Lindberg's wonderful luck, but determine to emulate Lindy's glorious pluck."[11]

In an editorial titled simply "Duty," Johnson expressed a view reminiscent of the Stoicism of the ancient Romans. He saw duty as a "hard task-master," a "relentless hand" driving men through trials that seemed intolerable. And yet, for those who followed the dictates of an "unrelenting discipline," there were ample rewards: "inward satisfaction . . . peace and happiness . . . fortitude and strength . . . self-reliance, unselfishness, poise, earnestness, and integrity." Johnson assured his fellow-

[10]*Ibid.*, September 27, 1927, p. 2.

[11]*Ibid.*, October 5, 1927, p. 2.

students that those who made duty "the controlling force of life" would find everyday tasks less distasteful and difficult, future plans for service easier to accomplish, and life more worth-while.[12]

Writing on a subject which has long fascinated college editorial writers, Lyndon Johnson discussed "Personality," which he defined as "identity, the sum total of one's personal characteristics." "Personality," he said, "is power; the man with a striking personality can accomplish greater deeds in life than a man of equal abilities but less personality." He wrote that personality was a combination of "altruistic feelings, noble purposes, talents and individuality." Each person, he said, should endeavor to acquire a "pleasing and effective personality." And he had a formula for its achievement: "unselfishness, originality, and concentrated effort; let us rise above the humdrum everyday ideas of life and build, carefully and wisely, real personalities." He concluded with a characteristic imperative: "Let your brow touch the sky. Force others to look up."[13]

Probably the most important editorial written by Lyndon Johnson while on the staff of the *Star,* in terms of foreshadowing the man who would become president, was his essay for Armistice Day, 1927. In it he showed how deeply imbued he was with the idealism of Woodrow Wilson. World War I was then nine years past; and Lyndon, only nineteen years old, had been a small boy during the conflict. He remembered the "terrific struggle" of that "long, agonizing conflict"; and he recalled the brave dead who gave their lives. "The most we can do to honor our heroes is all too little when weighed against the price they paid," he wrote. But Johnson wished to draw some positive lessons from the war. "We must not forget the things for which it was fought." It was a war to make the world safe for democracy, not just for the United States, but for all mankind. Apparently, he had caught much of Woodrow Wilson's visionary dream of world democracy and thus told his fellow-students that "by our words and deeds, we must foster brotherhood and democracy—democracy of thought and feeling, of principles and action." He saw World War I as a "war to honor law"—to make treaties more

---

[12]*Ibid.,* October 26, 1927, p. 2.
[13]*Ibid.,* November 9, 1927, p. 2.

than "mere scraps of paper." It was "a struggle to uphold the majesty and power of law." He advanced the idea that, although breaking the law was wrong before the war, it was much more so after it because "the law-breaker today ... violates not only the laws of God and man, but heedlessly scorns the precious privileges so dearly bought by the life-blood of soldiers in that mighty struggle for law-supremacy." Returning to the theme of a war to end all wars, the young Lyndon wrote a memorable paragraph which reads like some of his later presidential addresses:

Let us promote the cause of peace—a peace so dearly bought, so bravely gained, so anxiously awaited. Let there be no more of contention, of combat, of foolish strife and warring words. Let us unite in the attempt to secure the best for our nation and our people, making high ideals, instead of selfish gain and prideful ambition, our goal.[14]

As the fall holiday season approached in 1927, Johnson's thoughts turned to home and the meaning of the holidays. In an editorial on "Thanksgiving Day" he pictured what to him would be a perfect Thanksgiving: "eating Mother's turkey and basking in her smile and talking politics with Dad." And he took this opportunity to express his thanks for several things— the American home with "the care and affection of loving and wise parents, the championship of sturdy brothers and gentle sisters," American education, especially schools like Southwest Texas, and the privilege of being a citizen of the "greatest democratic government in the world."[15] Upon his return from the holidays, Johnson, suspecting there might be a let-down in studying during the period between Thanksgiving and Christmas, called upon his fellow-students to keep their standards high so that they could enjoy their Christmis holiday without a "twinge of conscience."[16]

In early December, 1927, the young writer penned an editorial called "The Cynic" which reflected an already-developed philosophy of life which was positive and activist. In this and

---

[14]*Ibid.*, November 16, 1927, p. 2.
[15]*Ibid.*, November 23, 1927, p. 2.
[16]*Ibid.*, November 30, 1927, p. 2.

other articles Johnson showed great admiration for Benjamin Franklin who, according to the young editor, was a reluctant revolutionist whose greatest contribution was to help build a workable government after the revolution was over. In contrast, Paine was an eager, almost a professional, revolutionist who condemned the new government wrought by Franklin and others and went off to France to fight another revolution. The two men presented a contrast between a doctrinaire and a practical man, between a radical and a moderate, between a man who knew only how to keep revolutions going and one who knew when to stop them. To the young Johnson, the difference was quite simple: one was a "destroyer," the other a "builder." "What will you be," he asked, "a builder or a destroyer? A constructor or a smasher of ideas?"[17]

The following month, Johnson returned to his consideration of Franklin on the occasion of his birthday. Johnson wrote that the history and Constitution of the United States had been affected by the "wisdom, good sense, and prudence of this virile and many-sided character." Franklin, he said, had contributed greatly to American independence with his diplomatic accomplishments in France. He had been the only man to sign all four of the significant documents in the formative period of the nation, including the Declaration of Independence and the Constitution. He also had been ambassador to France, governor of Pennsylvania, and first Postmaster General, as well as scientist, author, printer, editor, philosopher, inventor, humanitarian, practical man of affairs, and scholar. Johnson called Franklin "the most remarkable man of his time—in fact, one of the greatest men of this or any other nation."[18]

Another of Lyndon Johnson's editorials on the common virtues was one called "Vision." He said that vision gave inspiration to an artist to portray beauty on a canvas, allowed an architect to put into a set of blue-prints the beauty of a future building, and "upheld" statesmen in the framing of laws according to a vision of ideal government. Behind all constructive work was "a vision, a dream, a plan." Johnson was amazed at the criticism

[17]*Ibid.*, December 7, 1927, p. 2.
[18]*Ibid.*, January 18, 1928, p. 2.

directed at the dreams of youth. He did not regard all of them as laudable; but he felt that to young people came "the great visions, the masterly conceptions of achievements for which the world waits, the glowing ideals of work." Then came the imperative: "Let us hold to the vision granted us, and hold fast the truth it teaches."[19]

In the spring of 1928, when the time came for the annual freshman edition of the *College Star*, Johnson was still a freshman; and because of his extensive experience on the *Star*, he was the obvious choice to be its editor-in-chief. As was the custom, the freshmen printed their issue on green paper. It was dedicated to a young English instructor, Leland Derrick, now graduate dean and vice-president of Southwest Texas State. A banner headline announced that the *Pedagog* of 1927 had won national recognition from a publication known as *The Scholastic Editor*, and on the front page was a large picture of the beloved Old Main building. A special feature of the edition was a section called "A Glance Ahead." Editor Johnson had asked various faculty and students "whose acquaintance with the past of the college qualified them to pass mature judgment upon the affairs of the institution" to predict what was in store for Southwest Texas during the coming year. President Evans spoke of expansion of the physical plant; Dean Nolle talked of admission of Southwest Texas State graduates to good graduate schools as an encouraging sign; Dean of Women Brogdon looked forward to a "broader and merrier social program;" the registrar mentioned increased enrollment; the various coaches spoke optimistically but cautiously about the prospects for their teams; ex-football captain Alfred Johnson expressed his satisfaction with the choice of captains for the next year; and several department heads spoke of their plans for the new year.

The principal editorial of the freshman edition on "Will Power" was obviously the work of Lyndon Johnson although it had no by-line. It began by saying that high ideals alone were not enough to "carry forward a noble intention." Johnson continued:

There must be not only the desire to do, the impulse to create,

---

[19]*Ibid.,* February 1, 1928, p. 2.

but the strong determination to realize the ideal. The great men of the world are those who have never faltered. They had the glowing vision of a noble work to inspire them to press forward, but they also had the inflexible will, the resolute determination, the perfectly attuned spiritual forces for the execution of the work planned.

Then Johnson expressed some interesting and novel ideas about successful men and the interplay of noble impulses and will power:

The successful man has a well-trained will. He has under absolute control his passions and desires, his habits and his deeds. This strong will has made of the man a consistent, forceful character. He of the weak and uneducated will is swayed, first by this noble impulse and then by this baser one; his emotions control him. His will springs to do the bidding of this impulse only to be re-called by another impulse of a different order. His character is unstable, vacillating, and inferior.

Johnson called on his readers to "be diligent" in developing "true ideals, correct habits, and rigid self-control." Character, he said, comes from "the perfectly educated will"; it is the one worth-while achievement in life, far greater than riches, fame, or tri-umphs. Johnson ended with the characteristic remark that ed-ucation of the will is a continuous and unremitting task, but that it would reward those who achieve it "ten-thousand fold" in the future.[20]

In the spring of 1928 Lyndon turned his attention to teaching, which he called in an editorial "The Greatest of Vocations." By the end of the summer quarter he would com-plete two years of college work, making him eligible to teach in Texas public schools. He applied for a "two-year certificate," which he received on June 1, 1928. He then applied for a teach-ing job at Cotulla and accepted a position there for the school year 1928-29. Like most students at Southwest Texas, he was pre-paring for a teaching career and had completed five courses in education: introductory psychology, the teaching of arithmetic, classroom management, educational psychology, and the psychol-ogy of adolescence.[21] In his editorial Johnson detailed his phi-

[20]*Ibid.*, March 14, 1928, p. 2.
[21]College transcript of Lyndon B. Johnson.

losophy of education, reflecting some of the things he had been taught at the college. He said that the first duty of the teacher was to impart knowledge, a function of "great constructive influence." He then spoke of the rewards of teaching:

To lead inquiring and impressionable minds into the great treasure house of the knowledge that the world has accumulated is of itself a priceless privilege. To be of service to humanity is recompense for struggling years and patient study.

Great as was the privilege of instilling knowledge, it was surpassed by that of inspiring the love of knowledge. The ideal teacher, he wrote,

. . . is not only an efficient instructor, but a valiant crusader leading a quest for rare and precious treasures. . . . He leads the student to love learning for its own sake, as well as to appreciate it for the powers and advancements its acquiring brings.[22]

April 21 is San Jacinto Day in Texas, a holiday to celebrate Texas independence from Mexico and the victory of the Texas army of Sam Houston over General Santa Anna. In an editorial Johnson paid homage to Sam Houston and his "dauntless little band" who defeated the Mexicans in the swamp near Houston in twenty short minutes. It was a deed "so marvelously far-reaching and strikingly momentous that the whole world paused in astonishment." "No paeans of praise," or "showers of appreciation" could be too great for the heroes of San Jacinto.[23]

In an editorial titled "The Advantage of College Training," he outlined what he thought the advantages to be. One was better preparation of the duties of life, and another was acquiring "open-mindedness." Johnson felt that the atmosphere and associations of college life, as well as studies and activities, tended to "broaden the vision and open the mind." The college experience gave a student the ability, moreover, to place himself "in the other fellow's position." It also made him flexible: a college-trained person did not adhere strongly to doctrines, creeds, or dogmas simply because he had been taught to believe them. The college experience would make him tolerant enough to lis-

[22]*College Star,* April 18, 1928, p. 2.
[23]*Ibid.,* April 25, 1928, p. 2.

ten to the other side with an open mind; and even though the "college-bred man" might not see a good reason to alter an opinion, he would allow and respect the opposing view. The cultivation of broadmindedness, said Johnson, was the "genuine underlying purpose of education," and he admonished his fellow-students to make the best of their college opportunities.[24]

Continuing with his series of editorials on "the great virtues of life," Johnson discussed "Sincerity." He said that truly great men had always exhibited this virtue. Lincoln was a good example: "He was a homely, ungainly figure from the backwoods, and he never tried to present himself as anything else." And yet he captured the American imagination "not only because of the pathos of his life, but because of his sincerity." Lincoln, said Johnson, never lost the "feeling of his native soil"; and, in a passage particularly significant, wrote:

When Lincoln arrived at the Presidency, the way was open to him to put on a front and to do some strutting. Instead, he remained plain Abe Lincoln. No voice had to warn him to be himself. He was himself.

Somehow, Johnson continued, the world seemed to recognize sincerity and was quick to see hypocrisy. "If you believe in a thing, stand up for it. If you support a principle, give all you have to give. If you think a thing is wrong, do not waiver if you find that sentiment is against you." Vacillation in the face of criticism was the sign of weakness. In conclusion, Johnson maintained that one could be only himself. "You are you. Be honest with yourself. Be yourself!"[25]

Before the end of the spring quarter of 1928, the student council met and selected the editors of the *College Star* for the next year. They also chose Lyndon Johnson to be summer editor—quite an honor for a sophomore and also a welcome financial aid, since the job paid thirty dollars a month. In a front-page story the *Star* announced the new editors and gave a short biography of each. Concerning Johnson, the article said that he was a student of high scholastic standing, "well liked," and the first sophomore ever to be made editor of the college paper.

---

[24]*Ibid.*, May 2, 1928, p. 2.
[25]*Ibid.*, May 16, 1928, p. 2.

It explained that he had been on the editorial staff for two years and added that he was a "star member of the college debating squad" and was working his way through college as assistant secretary in the president's office.[26]

In the first edition of the paper under Johnson's editorship, the staff asked for the cooperation of the student body and promised to try to live up to the slogan "The News on Time." It also contained an editorial by the editor-in-chief on "Freedom." Everyone from "red revolutionists to conscientious reformers," he wrote, protested that they were in bondage and demanded freedom, but freedom was not simply lawlessness and rebellion: "Freedom recognizes the restrictions of law. The disciple of liberty understands that freedom is based upon the guaranteed rights of all." Johnson continued that a man was free only if he understood that freedom comes from within and is dependent upon self-mastery. He concluded:

There are no tyrannies like those human passions and weaknesses exercise. No master is so cruelly exacting as an indulged appetite. To govern self is a greater feat than to control armies and forces. . . . The liberty-loving soul rises above the petty restrictions of daily life and the oppression of custom. He is free, because he is master of himself and of all those forces within himself which control his individual freedom. He who chooses may be free.[27]

In the succeeding issue Johnson took up the subject of "Success," which he described as the goal of all: "the dream of youth, the passion of maturity, and the fond retrospect of the aged." It was, by Johnson's definition, "the attainment of that which is strongly desired." Wealth, prestige, position, power, honors, favors—all of these were manifestations of success. But success was more: it was living a life which was a blessing to humanity. A successful man was one who could lose sight of self "in the struggle for the good of humanity." The things that determined a man's success or failure were these: "the purpose animating his life, the ideals he cherished, the faith and perseverence he possesses." Success was seen by Johnson as "the triumph of the best and noblest potentialities of the individual . . . the achieve-

[26]*Ibid.*, June 6, 1928, p. 1.
[27]*Ibid.*, p. 2.

ment of his highest powers, his greatest service to mankind, his supreme development." And it was within the reach of all who would "plan carefully and unselfishly, determine wisely and firmly, and press forward resolutely and steadfastly to win it."[28]

In his next edition Johnson changed the format of the editorial page. Formerly, there had been one or two rather long editorials, but now there was to be a series of short ones written for the most part by Lyndon Johnson. In one of these he wrote that humor added "savor to the literary dish of college news," but he condemned the "coarse suggestiveness or immoral jokes which some college sheets seem to regard as humorous." In another item he called for the creation of a department of journalism at the college so that those who sought to learn the "hows and whys of editorial art" could do so. A third editorial pointed out that the college graduate, despite his degree, must be prepared to "start at the bottom" on his first job and work up. There were also a few remarks about the responsibilities of journalists, in which Johnson said they must see that news was "clean, important, and free from any tinge of propaganda." He added, ". . . in such a liberty-loving nation as ours the citizens should be given only the facts untinged by prejudice or propaganda and allowed to form their own opinions. This is an ideal for newspaper journalism."[29]

Johnson's preoccupation with journalism may be explained by events taking place not far away. About this time the Democratic National Convention was meeting in Houston. Johnson persuaded a friend with a car to drive him to Houston where he induced convention officials to admit him as a member of the press by producing copies of the *College Star* listing him as editor-in-chief. He also managed to get tickets for the friend with the car and for two girl friends. Johnson was at the convention for several days; and when he returned to the campus, he had to go before Dean Nolle to explain his absences. The dean recalled years later how excitedly the young man described his experiences at the national convention.[30]

[28]*Ibid.*, June 13, 1928, p. 2.
[29]*Ibid.*, June 20, 1928, p. 2.
[30]Interview with Alfred H. Nolle, San Marcos, November 13, 1964.

Johnson's attendance at the Democratic Convention has given rise to some recent journalistic errors. An Associated Press story in 1963, which was carried in many newspapers throughout the country, told how Johnson had obtained admission to the press gallery with copies of the *College Star* and intimated that he had been preparing for this moment by writing articles about the coming convention. It quoted some of the *Star* headlines: "Houston Convention Approaching" and "Democrats Converge on Houston,"[31] but no such stories or headlines appeared in the college newspaper. Under Johnson's editorship during June and July of 1928, the *Star* confined itself entirely to campus news stories, the only mention of the convention in Houston was a brief paragraph in his editorial column which is quoted here in its entirety:

Customs change, but principles are constant. Circumstances and time have no power to affect true and underlying principles. A splendid demonstration of this great truth was manifested in the Democratic National Convention at Houston. Issues of the hour were of less importance than the great party principles laid down by Thomas Jefferson, further outlined by Andrew Jackson, and later exemplified by Grover Cleveland and Woodrow Wilson. An issue comes and goes; a principle remains through the ages.[32]

In the weeks that followed, he wrote on many subjects. In "The Duties of Citizenship" he stated that it was the duty of the citizens to vote and to vote intelligently, to study the issues, review past records, and know the candidates and platforms. Johnson concluded:

One learns his duty to the state and nation, to humanity and to God, by a careful study of history and government. The past is an index to the future, and we determine our actions today by studying the effect of the deeds of our forefathers. If one would be a true citizen, he must study his constitution, learn his country's history, and study the biographies of the nation's heroes.[33]

In another piece he discussed the Democratic primary in Texas in which victory was tantamount to election. Johnson wrote that as long as elections were waged "honestly and openly, on mat-

---

[31]Houston *Post*, December 6, 1963, p. 3.

[32]*College Star*, July 11, 1928, p. 2.

[33]*Ibid.*, July 18, 1928, p. 2.

ters of principle and service to humanity," it was right for people to campaign with zeal and enthusiasm. He added, "A warm political battle, intensely but cleanly waged, is inspiring and worthy of the interest, aid, and concern of all true citizens." Johnson also noted that it was a matter of vital importance who was chosen for public office, and that voters should give careful consideration to the integrity, ability, and strength of candidates. Johnson also had some good words for the profession of politics. He felt that too often politicians were referred to "in a slurring manner." The real politician, he said, "is a patriot, a statesman, a student of governmental affairs, issues, and demands of the hour," not a "demagogue or a political trickster." A *politician,* in its true meaning, was one who understood "the science of government." If a good citizen learned to understand "the needs of people, the power and strength of the government, and the meaning and purpose of the law," he became a politician.[34]

An essay which indicated how Lyndon Johnson's political thought had matured by the age of twenty was entitled "The First American Assembly," which he wrote to commemorate the first colonial assembly at Jamestown in 1619. He said that this occasion was the beginning of "representative" government in the "greatest democracy in the world." Johnson maintained that it was the principle of representative democracy which had made America great. It had also made the United States a pattern for other nations, "a protector of the oppressed, a glorious leader of democracy in the world." In addition, it had developed individual citizenship to a "superlatively high degree." "America has made men," he wrote, "while other nations were creating mere subjects." Americans were "independent thinkers, loyal patriots, and the best citizens in the universe"; and all of this had been accomplished by representative government.[35]

While he was summer editor in 1928, Johnson instituted a new feature which was called "Who's Who in College World" and which consisted of photographs and biographical sketches of prominent faculty members. The first article quite naturally dealt with President C. E. Evans. Stories on the three deans—

[34]*Ibid.,* August 1, 1928, p. 2.
[35]*Ibid.*

Nolle, Brogdon, and Speck—appeared the following week. Then came short essays on Bryan Wildenthal, the business manager; E. B. Jackson, the librarian; and H. M. Greene, a government professor.[36]

As the summer session drew to a close, the editor of the *Star* prepared his final editorials, one of which dealt with the purpose of education. Johnson said that the growing interest in education in the United States stemmed from an increased desire on the part of young people to be of service. "Education," he wrote, "is the open door to service . . . it discovers one's abilities, cultivates and perfects them, thus rendering them capable of bringing service to the world." College students, he continued, wanted to be of service as scientists, doctors, lawyers, and teachers; and education would bring "the fruition of their hopes." It was an inspiring thing to be a part of "that great army of workers in training who shall shortly enter the ranks of skilled workers, serving humanity with the best abilities that education can give." In a closely related editorial he described the plans and preparations which had been made for the next school year; and he urged his fellow students to resume their education in September. By so doing, they would "greatly facilitate" the realization of their "laudable ambitions" to obtain a good education. Johnson praised Southwest Texas State as a "splendid school," and said that it was the best and most economical college available.[37]

Then, in an editorial titled "Farewell," he took leave of the *Star* as editor—but not permanently. He said he had "greatly enjoyed" his work, and he thanked all who had helped in the preparation, printing, and distribution of the paper. It was a sentimental moment; he wrote:

We are attached to the *Star,* and feel that we are giving up something personal in placing it in other hands. The sadness of our parting is relieved by the knowledge that we are resigning our beloved paper into the hands of a capable and loyal staff fired by the college spirit that has been the animus of our efforts.[38]

But despite his exhortations to fellow-students to return for

[36]*Ibid.,* August 1, 8, 18, 1928.

[37]*Ibid.*

[38]*Ibid.,* August 18, 1928, p. 2.

the academic year, Lyndon Johnson was not able to do so himself. Financial necessities forced him, like many Southwest Texas State students, to take a job teaching after he had finished his first two years of college. For the next nine months he taught at Cotulla in South Texas; but in the summer of 1929 he followed his own good advice, returned to the campus at San Marcos to continue his education, and was chosen again as editor of the college newspaper. In his first editorial he expressed some of his impressions about changes in the college which had taken place in his absence. He wrote that the campus was growing, with the addition of several new "valuable and attractive buildings"; that the faculty was strong and increasing in numbers; and that the pride which the students felt in their alma mater had kept pace with the growth. He was not happy, however, to find that, although the curriculum had been "broadened and strengthened," a school of journalism was still lacking. In the same issue of the newspaper, Johnson stated in a few words some of the ideas he had expressed many times before:

> The world today is looking for men who are not for sale;
> Men who are masters of themselves and their tempers;
> Men who place principle above all else;
> Men who are honest and true;
> Men who love work and the contentment it brings;
> Men who are willing to lose sight of self, ease, and
>   pleasure in the effort to serve others.[39]

Two other short items written during the summer of 1929 are of special interest in the light of subsequent events. The first had to do with the role of education in promoting a composite nationality:

Sectionalism is vanishing. Our nation is becoming more truly American. One great factor in the wiping out of sectional ties is the education of the masses. Our colleges and universities are accomplishing a great work in creating not Northerners, Southerners, Easterners or Westerners, but Americans.

The second is equally significant:

Ambition is an uncomfortable companion many times. He creates a discontent with present surroundings and achievements; he is

---

[39]*Ibid.*, June 12, 1929, p. 2.

never satisfied but always pressing forward to better things in the future. Restless, energetic, purposeful, it is ambition that makes of a creature a real man.[40]

Through the long hot summer of 1929 Lyndon Johnson stayed faithfully at his typewriter and poured out a steady stream of material for his columns. Almost every week he warned his readers that time was slipping by, and he admonished them to take advantage of the great opportunities available at Southwest Texas State College. Among the editorials that followed, two read as if they had been written by a man who would one day become one of the hardest working presidents in history. In one he wrote, "Work is the best antidote for that poison called worry." Many times, he said, the cause of worry was imagined; but real or imagined, worry served no useful purpose and the best cure for it was work. In the other brief essay he stated that one of the best advantages of the summer session of college was that it "banishes idleness." He said some students might think it too great a burden to go to school throughout the year, but he made it clear that it was foolish to fritter away a whole summer by doing nothing. He wrote, "A busy time, a happy time, some play and some work, is the satisfying situation at S.W.T.S.T.C."

Johnson later discussed the difficulty of facing new problems and challenges. He said that to face the unknown with its possible terrors required "courage of a high order," but that those who did it were the benefactors of humanity. He urged: "Suppress your fear of the new and the untried; step out from the ranks of neophobia sufferers and promptly, eagerly make any change that will make for your advancement and that of your fellow-man."

On another theme Johnson wrote, "What you accomplish in life depends almost completely upon what you make yourself do." He said that if a man wished strongly enough for something, was willing to go through "all kinds of trials," and concentrated on "the essential . . . and discarded the frivolous and unimportant," he could achieve ultimate success. He added a memorable sentence: "The ability to control the mind perfectly and to direct

---

[40]*Ibid.*, June 19, 1929, p. 2.

its mental processes is seen to be of supreme importance in the making of a career, the shaping of a life work and any real accomplishment."

As students of American civilization know, it was quite common in the late 1920's for writers, usually called "debunkers," to publish biographies of famous men in history which revealed that the long-revered idols had feet of clay. Lyndon Johnson condemned this practice and wrote, "the great have their weaknesses, but for these weaknesses to be magnified and exploited works no good to the reading public." He pointed out that hero worship was a "tremendous force in uplifting and strengthening humanity" and added:

Let us have our heroes. Let us continue to believe that some have been truly great; that it lies within human ability to overcome temptations and trials; that it is sublime to suffer and be strong. Petty biographers with inferior souls and jealous hearts would rob us of these happy privileges. Sensationalism is all right for yellow journalism, but in biography we wish to see our famous men and women as they were and feel the power of the strength and beauty of their lives. Down with the debunking biographer.[41]

In the next-to-last issue of the *Star* under Johnson's editorship there appeared an essay by him of such literary quality and quotability that it is reproduced here. It was called "The Enemy of Ignorance":

When we say that Truth is the inveterate enemy of error and its train of evil, we say that it is the foe of ignorance also.

It is in the darkness of ignorance that intolerance grows, with its awful brood of prejudice, persecution and strife.

It is ignorance that makes it necessary to veil the Truth to many if we would have them accept it.

All down the ages those who have known have had to suffer martyrdom in order to save from themselves those who did not know.

It is those who believe in witches, "bad luck" signs, and other similarly silly things who are most intolerant. The more ignorant one is, the more infallibly certain he feels himself to be in matters about which he has convictions.

It is in the garden where the cultivating hand of skill and knowledge never comes that we find most weeds.

The ignoramus is fanatical in his zeal in promoting his fallacies.

---

[41]*Ibid.*, July 17, 1929, p. 2.

This accounts for the fact that those who have undertaken to push forward the Truth and intellectual and spiritual development have to suffer most.

False education is the most dangerous ignorance.

That is, education based upon false assumptions and untrue statements is the greatest menace. It instills the idea into the minds of those who receive it that they are farther from the truth than are those who do not claim to know anything of the matter under consideration.

Notwithstanding, those who have love for humanity at heart, who have visions of what is best for human happiness and try to impart it to others, often have to suffer for their wisdom and foresight; still they at last are happier to follow the urge of their inspiration.

And this despite the fact that they soon will be forgotten after their sacrifice. It was so in the past and now.[42]

Turning his attention to the subject of selfishness, Johnson wrote that there was a form of selfishness more sordid than love of money. It was the refusal to do "goodly deeds," to speak encouraging words, or to manifest sympathetic interest in the misfortunes of others. Johnson believed that "those endowed with genius" had a duty to make their talents available to everyone. He wrote, "Glorious as is genius, it is of little value unless it is wisely and practically applied for the comfort and welfare of mankind." In the same way, a man of talent must use his gift in the interest of humanity or it was wasted, and a man of wealth had a duty to make his money useful.[43]

The final issue of the *Star* with Lyndon Johnson as editor came on August 14, 1929. In his editorial policy Johnson had always leaned toward big headlines on the front page, even though the event described might not seem to warrant it. An example was one which went all across the front page in block letters: "College Theater to Present Medieval Play." For his final issue, however, Johnson outdid himself. In letters three inches high, unheard of in the *Star,* he proclaimed, "Cage Captain Weds." Weddings were nothing new at Southwest Texas, and very likely this headline was Lyndon Johnson's own private joke. The cage captain who had wed was Merrell "Blackie" Blackman, a star basketball player, a Black Star, and a close friend of Lyndon Johnson's. His bride

---

[42]*Ibid.,* August 7, 1929, p. 2.
[43]*Ibid.*

was Miss Mazie Oaks of Bebe, Texas. Johnson was best man. There was no attempt at humor in describing the wedding; it was a straight account in great detail. The only humorous part was the huge headline, which was probably Lyndon Johnson's wedding present to his friend.[44]

Johnson's final editorials were quite significant. One was called "The Dollar's Soliloquy." If a dollar were to speak, according to Johnson, it would say that, although it held no intrinsic value, it was useful in the affairs of man. It could be used for good or evil, depending on how men wanted to use it. Johnson quoted the dollar as saying, "I would rather set free than enslave, to extend aid than to oppress, to construct than destroy, to give comfort than to make miserable, to cause joy than sorrow." The dollar, he asserted, was the slave of the generous man and the master of the avaricious one. He wanted dollars to be used to make children laugh with toys and to provide "pretty white beds for them to sleep in, and dainty white covers for them to sleep under"; he would rather see dollars spent to build a hundred comfortable houses for needy families than one big palace for a stingy, selfish man. He wanted dollars to be used to promote justice and protect law-abiding citizens, to build churches rather than prisons, hospitals rather than bagnios. Money, he said, was not dirty—it was "filthy lucre" and "tainted" only when men made it so. It was true that money talks, but men supplied the words.

Lyndon Johnson's last editorial was prophetic. Written thirty-five years before anyone ever heard of "The Great Society," it contained definite overtones of that ideal:

Today, intellectually America is fast asleep! With all our boasted wealth and material advance, we are living educationally in a dark age.

But there is a new day coming in America, when schoolboys will find new joy that captures and thrills them in discovering and developing their own native capacities, quite as much as in baseball or football, when achievements in nobility, and in creative living, in making friends and in holding them, will crowd crime off the front pages of our newspapers.

When college students will talk in dead earnest, yes, sometimes all night, about economics, politics, chemistry, and vastness of space, the limits of time, mathematics, literature, biology, and religion.

---

[44]*Ibid.*, August 14, 1929, p. 1.

When great monuments will be erected to teachers as creators of significant life; when our school and university buildings will be like cathedrals in their dignity and beauty, and wealth will deem itself honored to endow them.

A day when, at last, America, with its mighty resources and dormant brain and soul power, will actually be awake and up, done with intellectual sleepwalking, and a giant in spirit as well as body![45]

The editorials of Lyndon Johnson, spanning a period of more than two years, show the development of a young but surprisingly mature mind. They give evidence that his knowledge and understanding had been deepened and enriched by his college experience. His basic principles, however, had remained unchanged. At the present time, the editorials may seem a bit too florid and moralistic, but there can be no doubt that the able young man who wrote them had great ambition, determination, and intellectual capacity, qualities he had already revealed as a teacher in Cotulla.

---

[45]*Ibid.,* August 14, 1929, p. 2.

VII.

JOHNSON, THE TEACHER

1

LOCATED APPROXIMATELY MIDWAY BETWEEN SAN ANTONIO TO the north and Laredo to the south on a highway that runs from Dallas to Mexico City, Cotulla is the sun-baked capital of a broad expanse of flat, treeless brush country called the Nueces Plains, where ranching is the major occupation and the trailer hitch a recognizable status symbol. It is a dry, hot land with horizons which seem to extend to the ends of the earth and where infrequent rains often come in torrents, flooding the normally lazy streams and settling the wandering dust back to earth. Its people are warm and friendly in a way characteristic of ranchers and those who wrestle daily with the vagaries of weather and cattle. They do not pretend to be anything but what they are; indeed, on any ordinary day the uninitiated would find it difficult to distinguish the banker from the cattleman or the prosperous merchant from the cowhand, for the mark of the male citizen is a broad-brimmed hat, an open shirt, and cowboy boots and pants. Such apparel is not affectation. In one way or another, as owner, manager, or ranch hand, there are few in Cotulla who are not in some way involved in the cattle industry or who do not aspire to be.

Scorching hot in the summer sun, mercifully cool in the shade where the prevailing breezes fan the perspiration, Cotulla is magnificent at night, with nothing to obscure one hundred and eighty degrees of starlight except an occasional thunderhead which dissipates almost as quickly as it forms. During the winter the town lies open to the blasts of northers which sweep uninhibited out of Canada across the vast plains of the Central United States into Northern Mexico. Sudden changes of temperature are then characteristic of the region although the climate is moderate compared with that of the flat areas farther north.

In 1928 the population of the town was roughly three thousand, more than seventy-five per cent of whom were of Latin-American descent. It contained slightly fewer than half of the total residents of La Salle County and was then as now its only urban area.[1] The Missouri Pacific Railroad split the town approximately in half with Main Street paralleling the tracks to the west. Despite the later construction of a new highway which caused some business houses to move their location and others to be built, the original area today remains vigorous and central to the town's business life. The bulk of population lay east of the tracks; but the railroad as a demarcation line between the Latin and Anglo communities was less pronounced thirty-six years ago than it is today, the town having expanded westward with the coming of new residents and the rising level of prosperity.

When Lyndon Baines Johnson arrived in September, 1928, to begin his teaching career, many local citizens, along with millions of other Americans, were deeply interested in the presidential race between Alfred E. Smith and Herbert Hoover, a

---

[1]*Fifteenth Census of the United States: 1930.* "Population," III, pt. 2. United States Department of Commerce, Bureau of the Census, U. S. Government Printing Office (Washington, 1932). Table 16, p. 1010.

contest that sparked political controversy all over the South, with particularly sharp repercussions in Texas. No issue created greater division in the Democratic Party than the argument over prohibition, and during the campaign a strong anti-Smith movement developed which precipitated a bitter fight with the party regulars at the State Democratic Convention in mid-September. When anti-Smith delegates were refused recognition by the party leaders, fist fights broke out between the two factions; the rebuffed delegates walked out, organized a rump convention, and adopted a resolution scoring the regulars and Al Smith but endorsing the state administration. Controversy and political activity continued unabated until after the election in November, which Hoover won by an overwhelming majority, the Republicans carrying the state for the first time since the Reconstruction Era.

Preoccupation with politics was halted briefly, however, in October by the World Series and the outstanding performance of one of the great baseball heroes of all time. Babe Ruth, reported the Cotulla *Record,* climaxed his career by hitting three home runs in the last game of the series at St. Louis and made a sensational one-hand catch, ending the game. The Yankees, the newspaper continued, had won eight straight World Series games, "a record that will probably hold for a hundred years to come."[2] Those for whom baseball held no interest could reaffirm their belief that prosperity was here to stay by reflecting on the announcement of Henry Ford that his company was selling five thousand cars a day; and prohibitionists, concerned over the stand of Al Smith, found the views of W. C. Durant, prominent automobile manufacturer and Wall Street figure, reassuring. Prohibition, he declared, was successful; and he offered $25,000 to the author of the best and most practicable plan to make the country bone dry, the winner to be announced on Christmas Day.[3]

Prominently reported in the weekly newspaper and of considerable local interest was the opening of the Cotulla schools. Among the faculty members who assembled on September 10, 1928, was Lyndon Johnson, armed with a two-year elementary school certificate issued to him in June, 1928, but without a

---

[2]Cotulla *Record,* October 12, 1928, p. 1.

[3]Cotulla *Record,* September 6, 1928, p. 5; September 13, 1928, p. 2.

Lyndon Baines Johnson, Principal

college degree.[4] Needing money to complete his college work
and wanting experience, he had accepted, at the end of his soph-

[4]*Register of Teachers Certificates, 1928-29,* County Superintendent's Office, La
Salle County.

omore year at Southwest Texas State Teachers College in San Marcos, an offer to become principal of Welhausen Ward School, which had been opened two years earlier for Latin-American children. He was twenty years old, tall and slim, handsome, and, according to those who knew and worked with him, surprisingly mature for his age. His salary was to be $1125 for nine months, a rather respectable sum during that era when the average annual income for male teachers in Texas was $842, when manual workers received from 33 to 58 cents an hour for a 65-hour week, and when the compensation of the governor of the state was $4000.[5]

The duties of the new principal included the supervision of five teachers, responsibility for the sixth and seventh grades, and management of the physical plant with the aid of Tomas Coronado, former ranch hand who became janitor when Welhausen was opened in 1926 and is still its custodian. From all accounts of colleagues and students alike, Johnson was a firm administrator, a strict disciplinarian, and a good teacher. He permitted only English to be spoken on the school grounds, as he was convinced that Mexican children living in a Texas community must learn the language; and he required constant adult supervision of the students during the school day. His students recall that failure to study and to perform in the classroom as well as on the playground was likely to bring some form of punishment. A hard worker himself, Johnson expected others to work with equal energy and determination. He was persistent, sometimes high-tempered, energetic, aggressive, and creative. Working under a superintendent disliked by some of his teachers, he loyally carried out his directives but devised ways to minimize interference from higher authorities. A former colleague remembers that upon the approach of the administrator, Johnson would hastily summon into his office a number of Latin-American men who often sat on the steps of Welhausen to exchange the latest bits of news, station them across from his desk, and engage them in animated conversation. The superintendent thus found his

[5]Statistical Abstract of the United States, 1930. United States Department of Commerce, Bureau of the Census (Washington, 1930), pp. 111, 339, 341; The American Year Book: A Record of Events and Progress for the Year 1929, edited by Albert S. Hart and William M. Schuyler (New York, 1930), 92.

principal seemingly involved in sober discussion with parents of students who were no doubt in some difficulty and was pleased to note that they were not only nodding agreement but emphasizing their approval by periodic expressions of "Sí, sí, Señor; sí, sí, Señor."[6]

Like most teachers in small schools where faculties frequently find themselves engaged in all kinds of activities not directly related to the classroom, Johnson was soon involved in numerous extra-curricular projects, some assigned by his superiors, most of them the product of his own initiative. At the first faculty meeting of all the teachers in the Cotulla schools, he was given the task of training debaters and extemporaneous speakers for participation in the Interscholastic League contests to be held later in the year.[7] He soon organized a class in debate and public speaking for high school students which met regularly after school, and he was named the sponsor of the literary society which he helped organize.

His main duties, however, were at Welhausen, where he developed a well-rounded program for the elementary school children similar in some respects to that conducted for high schools by the Interscholastic League. In regular assemblies students were given the opportunity to perform; and a field day, to which teams from the surrounding area were invited to participate in spelling, declamation, softball, track, and field events, was organized. Teams from Welhausen also went to other small towns in the region; and in arranging for these trips, Johnson exhibited a talent later to be developed to a high degree of efficiency, the ability to get others to help him achieve a goal which was of particular interest to him. Teachers and parents who owned automobiles were soon transporting the players to Millett, Los Angeles, Fowlerton, Encinal, and other nearby towns where base-

[6]Interview with Mary Wildenthal, primary teacher at Welhausen, now retired, Cotulla, August 10, 1964.

[7]Organized in 1910 as the Debating League of Texas High Schools, enlarged in 1911 and again in 1912, when athletic activities formerly directed by the Interscholastic Association were added, the University Interscholastic League by 1950 supervised more than fifty different events involving half a million students in the Texas public schools. Competition in some extends from local eliminations through district and regional contests to a final state championship; in others competition stops at lower levels. Roy Bedicheck, "University Interscholastic League," *Handbook of Texas* (Austin, 1952), II, 820.

ball and other contests were held. The return from these trips was frequently the occasion for celebration in which the team was treated to refreshments purchased by Coach Johnson from a small store located across the street from the school grounds. These contests, vividly remembered by former students, were discontinued within a few years after Johnson left because of the large amount of planning they required and the difficulty of providing transportation in the absence of busses, which were not acquired for the Mexican school until much later.

Although his duties at Welhausen occupied most of his time, Johnson continued to train the high school students in public speaking. To obtain as much information as he could on the Interscholastic League debate topic that year, he wrote his friend, E. B. Jackson, librarian at Southwest Texas State, requesting material.[8] Unfortunately, the library was not well equipped to provide much assistance on the rather difficult subject: "Resolved, that the English cabinet method of legislation is more efficient than the committee system in the United States";[9] and Jackson referred him to the Extension Bureau of the University of Texas. Despite the difficulty of obtaining pertinent material, however, his students did exceptionally well at the county meet in early April, sweeping all events in debate, extemporaneous speaking, and senior declamation. Neither the debaters nor the extemporaneous speakers survived the district competition, which was held later in the month at Uvalde; but Edward Talbott placed first in senior boys' declamation and Katherine Kuykendall second in the girls' division.[10]

These achievements, together with Johnson's performance as principal, merited him a renewal of his contract by the Cotulla School Board at the end of the spring term.[11] But he was eager to return to college and complete work on his degree, toward which he had earned twelve hours of credit during the year at the extension center established in Cotulla by Southwest Texas State Teachers College in the late summer of 1928. This center

---

[8]L.B.J. to E.B.J., January 3, 1929.

[9]Roy Bedicheck, *Educational Competition: The Story of the University Interscholastic League of Texas* (Austin, 1956), 480.

[10]San Antonio *Express*, April 15, 1929, p. 9.

[11]Cotulla *Record*, May 24, 1929, p. 1.

had been authorized to offer courses toward the Bachelor of Arts and Bachelor of Science degrees in education, history, sociology, economics, and religion. If these were satisfactorily completed, they would be accepted by all colleges and universities holding membership in the Southern Association.[12] Johnson's enormous energy extended not only to his many responsibilities at Welhausen and the high school, but also to enrollment in two courses at the center during each of the three quarters, for credit in educational psychology, community activities in the rural school, race relations, elementary economics, and the social teachings of Jesus, all of them taught by Superintendent W. T. Donaho.[13] Having saved enough money to complete his college work, Johnson returned to San Marcos in June, where he was continuously enrolled until August, 1930, when he was awarded the Bachelor of Science degree.

Recollections of former students, colleagues, and townspeople who knew the future president as a young teacher confirm later estimates of his major characteristics: a tremendous energy and capacity for work, the ability to persuade others to help him in various projects in which he was interested, great initiative in developing new and varied programs to broaden the experience of his students, an aggressive quality of leadership, and a deep sympathy for the varied problems which his Latin-American children encountered both culturally and economically. From all accounts he was strict but fair, worked extremely hard and expected others to do likewise, and did not spare the rod if he thought it was needed. Dan Garcia, successful businessman and member of the Cotulla City Council, remembers that he was disciplined by Johnson for misbehaving while the young principal was out of the room attending to administrative duties.[14] His students liked him and appreciated his interest in them and his genuine concern for their educational and physical welfare, and they rewarded him in his later career with their enthusiastic and loyal political support.

For Johnson the experience was equally rewarding. He saved enough money to return to college and at the same time gained

---

[12]*Ibid.*, August 30, 1928, p. 1.

[13]Records of Dr. Alfred H. Nolle, retired Dean of Southwest Texas State College.

[14]Interview with Dan Garcia, Cotulla, August 11, 1964.

additional credits toward the baccalaureate degree. Even more significant for the future, he gained an insight into the problems faced by children of culturally and economically deprived groups and a lasting concern for their welfare.

2

While Lyndon was in college and briefly in Cotulla as teacher and principal, his Uncle George Johnson was chairman of the history department at Sam Houston Senior High School in Houston. Situated fifty miles inland in an area rich in cotton, oil, rice, and lumber, and connected to the Gulf of Mexico by a man-made channel capable of handling ocean-going vessels, Houston was the largest city in Texas and destined to become its greatest metropolitan district. In 1930, one year after the collapse of the stock market, local optimism and pride and the competitive spirit still animated most of its nearly three hundred thousand residents; but the pinch of the Great Depression was beginning to be felt. The steadily lengthening breadlines were an increasingly difficult problem for city officials and an economic burden to local taxpayers and private charities. In December the city administration found it necessary to open a commissary supported by private subscriptions; but the drain on these resources by some four thousand destitute families during the winter forced Mayor Walter Monteith in April, 1931, to call for additional donations of $40,000 to finance public relief during the ensuing six or eight months.[15]

Salaried personnel, including teachers, felt the economic lash of the depression somewhat more slowly than did many less fortunate employees; but when reduction occurred, it was sharp and prolonged. George Johnson, for example, who earned $2800 as head of his department in 1931, was reduced to $2400 in 1932 and to $2232 in 1933 and, along with other teachers, did not regain the salary he had received at the onset of the depression until after the entrance of the United States into World War II in 1941.[16] With no income tax to pay, however, and no deductions for retirement, since Texas had no such plan for teachers,

---

[15]Houston *Press*, April 3, 1931, p. 1.

[16]*Board Minutes*, the Houston Independent School District, Book E, 121; Book F, 19, 101; Book G, 75; Book I, 77; Book J, 22.

George Johnson

he fared somewhat better than did many and was grateful to have a job at all.

George was a bachelor and lived with his sister, the former

Ava Lee Johnson, and her husband, John Bright, on Hawthorne Street.[17] He and the Brights had been close friends for many years, having been in Port Arthur and Beaumont together before George left to accept a teaching position in Houston. And it was George who was responsible for Bright's employment at Sam Houston to teach mathematics before being transferred to San Jacinto, a new high school opened in Houston several years later. George was a kind and affable man, popular with his students and associates, and capable of making warm and enduring friendships. Unobtrusively charitable, he extended to his students financial help and other assistance during the hard days of the depression. Tall, partially bald, with a flair for histrionics, he created a lasting impression upon those who knew him; and his death in the early 1940's deeply grieved his many students, friends, and relatives.

George's special interest was the history of the United States and, particularly, the age of Andrew Jackson, which he considered to be the most significant and generally agreeable period in our national development.[18] But he was also an assiduous student of Texas politics, which he viewed as fascinating and instructive. Anecdotes concerning various aspects of Texas history and its political development were frequently inserted into his classes and, being duly noted by his students in the margins of their textbooks, were passed on to later classes for use in jogging George's memory in case he neglected to recall them.

Of all contemporary politicians, George most admired Joseph Weldon Bailey of Texas, who served as national congressman from 1891 to 1901 and as senator from 1901 until he resigned in 1913. Bailey was one of the most dynamic men ever to stride into the arena of Texas politics, and his death in 1929 ended forty-five years of a vigorous and sometimes stormy career and signalled the beginning of the end of one of the most colorful eras in the political history of the state. Characterized as a "firebrand in Texas and national politics," Bailey was distinguished by his "picturesque dress, distinctive personality, and a gift of oratory, perhaps exceeded only by William Jennings Bryan," as

---

[17]The home is still occupied by one of the Bright daughters and her husband, Mr. and Mrs. A. C. Askew.

[18]Interview with Dorothea Bright Askew, Houston, August 15, 1964.

well as his mighty devotion to states' rights and his equally mighty opposition to prohibition and women's suffrage.[19] Described as a "Southerner born and bred" who, arrayed in a "dull black frock coat, flowing tie, and a big black, slouch hat," continually reaffirmed his belief in Jeffersonian Democracy, Bailey was a good friend of Bryan's and was credited by some with having "influenced the Great Commoner in the formulation of his most celebrated doctrines, among them the Bryan metal theroy."[20] A staunch and unshakable friend, an equally implacable foe, Bailey possessed some qualities, both political and personal, which would have elicited Andrew Jackson's admiration and respect. George revered him, often remarking on what a wonderful man Bailey was and frequently quoting from memory long passages from his many speeches.[21] He was, to George, the ideal politician, an estimate which he frequently expressed to his colleagues and friends, and to his nephew from Johnson City.

Shortly after his arrival at Sam Houston, George Johnson acquired the name of "Senator," not because of any political aspirations or involvement, but because of his periodic performances at student assemblies and pep rallies where his gestures reminded his audience of a "Senator on a soap box." Since Sam Houston had no auditorium at the time, announcements had to be made from a second-floor balcony overlooking an open court below where the students were assembled. Such an arrangement lent itself to the forensic skill of the speakers, and George made the most of the opportunities to display his talents and to demonstrate his genuine interest in the various student activities.

In addition to history and politics, George had other interests which stimulated his enthusiasm and devotion, the most important being the budding career of his nephew, Lyndon Johnson, soon to graduate from college with a Bachelor of Science degree and a permanent teaching certificate. Without children of his own, he centered his affections upon the two Bright daughters

---

[19]Dallas *Morning News*, April 14, 1929, pp. 1, 4, on the occasion of Bailey's death in Sherman, Texas, the day before. See also the San Antonio *Express*, April 14, 1929, pp. 1, 15; James A. Clark, *The Tactful Texan: A Biography of Governor Will Hobby* (New York, 1958), 22-23.

[20]San Antonio *Express*, April 14, 1929, pp. 1, 15.

[21]Interview with Byron Parker, colleague of George Johnson at Sam Houston, now retired, Houston, August 14, 1964.

and on Lyndon, about whom he talked often to his friends; he particularly enjoyed recounting his nephew's success as a college debater and expressing the hopes and ambitions he had for his future. "I never heard him tell Lyndon to get into politics," Byron Parker recalls; "but I did hear him say that 'if I were a young man like you, I'd run for congress.' "[22]

It was undoubtedly through his Uncle George that Lyndon became interested in teaching in Houston, where he applied for a job in the spring of his senior year. With teaching opportunities at a premium during the lean years of the early 1930's, George's position as department chairman might have weighed the scales in his nephew's favor, for on June 11, 1930, almost two months before Lyndon's graduation, the Houston School Board, acting on the recommendation of Superintendent E. E. Oberholtzer, hired him at an annual salary of $1600, to be assigned when a vacancy occurred.[23]

During the succeeding summer months, Lyndon Johnson completed work on his degree; and, as September approached and no opening had developed in Houston, he took a job at Pearsall, near Cotulla, as a teacher of public speaking. His tenure there was brief, however, for in late October he was notified by the Houston School Board of his appointment to the faculty of Sam Houston to teach debating and public speaking. He resigned his position at Pearsall, received a check for $67.00 for his services of little more than a month, and left immediately to assume his new duties.[24] More fortunate than most, Johnson already had an entree into faculty circles through his uncle as well as a place to live; he moved in with the Brights, where he shared a room with George during the entire time he taught in Houston, a period of about thirteen months.

In the fall of 1930 Sam Houston was one of five senior high schools in the city, with a faculty of seventy and a student body of almost seventeen hundred. Its location in the center of the downtown area drew students of varied economic and cultural

---

[22]*Ibid.*

[23]*Board Minutes,* The Houston Independent School District, Book E, 33.

[24]Records in Pearsall Superintendent's Office, John C. Waldrum, Curriculum Coordinator, Pearsall Public Schools, to E. C., September 21, 1964. His position was filled by his sister, Rebekah.

backgrounds, most of whom lived in the immediate vicinity and in the residential sections lying west of the business district. Despite the stringencies of the depression, many of the school's graduates went on to college and later became leaders in business and professional circles in Houston and throughout the state. At the head of the administration was William J. Moyes, a wise and humane scholar who was as knowledgeable in the writings of Cicero and Virgil as he was in operating a smoothly functioning high school and in understanding the problems and perplexities of his many students. An able principal and genuinely fine man, he earned the respect and devotion of all who knew him, whether as colleague or superior.

His faculty, many of whom earned master's degrees for which no added compensation was possible until after the depression lifted, was one of the best in the city. As Houston continued to grow and new residential areas developed, however, students formerly in the Sam Houston district were later transferred to new high schools; and teachers at old Central were gradually shifted to become the nucleus of the new faculties. Some who were teaching at Sam Houston in 1930 are still employed in the Houston system either as teachers or administrators; some have retired; many of them remember vividly the young, restless man who arrived on very short notice in early November to fill a vacancy in the speech department.

Johnson was twenty-two when he assumed his new duties and was still not absolutely certain what he wanted to do with his life. In an editorial written for the college newspaper three years before, he had described teaching "as one of the noblest if not the noblest [profession] in the world";[25] and again in 1928 he paid homage editorially to the great teachers who imparted to their students a love of learning and thus became immortal through their influence on future generations.[26] His own career as director of debate and teacher of public speaking was brief but distinguished, and he later remarked that his year in Houston had been one of the happiest of his life. But the attraction of politics was strong; and to many who knew him both in Cotulla

[25]"Higher Ideals," College Star, August 10, 1927.
[26]"The Greatest of Vocations," College Star, April 18, 1928.

and in Houston, he was a young man of restless energy and ambition who was "marking time" until a clearer vision of his own future came into focus. To Michael Spampinato, director of the Sam Houston band and language instructor, whose duties, like those of Lyndon's, kept him frequently after school. Johnson once revealed his doubts as they were walking home together: "I don't know whether I want to stay in teaching or not. I think I would like to get into politics."[27]

Whether or not Johnson intended to make teaching a career or was simply waiting for some opportunity to enter the political world, there is no doubt that he plunged immediately into his new job with great energy and enthusiasm. And his duties were augmented shortly after his arrival when he was assigned to teach public speaking in the Sam Houston night school—one of several which the school board had recently authorized—at the rate of $1.50 an hour.[28] He quickly established rapport with his students, who found him likeable but demanding of their time and energy and impatient with anything less than top performance. On one occasion, when he was congratulated by a fellow-teacher for the good sportsmanship exhibited by one of his students who had lost a debate, Lyndon replied: "I'm not interested in how they lose. I'm just interested in how they win."[29] "He worked the life out of them," another colleague recalls, "but they would do anything for him." Although he pushed them to maximum effort, she continued, he never used them for his own aggrandizement nor required of them more than he was willing to do himself.[30] His keen interest in student activities, which included assisting the cheerleaders at pep rallies on occasion, together with a pleasing personality, made him popular; but the line between teacher and student was always clearly drawn. Personable, dynamic, and self-assured, he seemed to attract people to him; and there was something about him that made them remember him, "whether it was the manner of his speech, or the things he said, or the way

---

[27]Interview with Michael Spampinato, Supervisor of Bands for the Houston Independent School District, Houston, August 17, 1964.

[28]*Board Minutes*, Houston Independent School District, Book E, 58, 67.

[29]Interview with Ruth Daugherty, Houston, August 14, 1964.

[30]Interview with Ellana Eastham Ball, Houston, October 24, 1964.

he laughed. I can always remember that, the hearty laugh and the way he shook his shoulders."[31]

Courses in public speaking had been offered at Sam Houston for several years prior to Johnson's arrival, and representatives of the school had occasionally won top honors in city and county competition, particularly in declamation; but debate was another matter. Here the field was dominated by teams from San Jacinto, arch-rival of Sam Houston and winner of the city championship for four consecutive years. To prepare his students for the usual round of debates with their traditional rivals, with other teams from the surrounding area, and for competition in the Inter-scholastic League, Johnson organized a series of inter-class contests, the winners of which would represent the school in the coming events. Normal effort and eagerness were intensified in early December when M. E. Foster, editor of the Houston *Press,* announced the donation of $100 in prizes to be awarded to the outstanding public speakers at Johnson's discretion. In commenting on the value of courses in debate and public speaking, Foster, better known as "Mefo," whose daily column *Why* became a by-word to Houston readers and to the newspaper world, wrote:

Haven't you seen men of high standing tremble and stammer when they tried to respond to some call upon them for a little talk? That's because they had no early training. They know the words but do not know how to use them. One method of encouraging boys and girls today to learn the advantages of a course in public-speaking is to offer prizes to high school debating classes. When you debate a question you learn to think quickly and express yourself clearly and forcibly. We need thinkers and speakers in the days to come. We need them now.

. . . we encourage the high school athlete. Why not one who can best his opponent in a mental test?[32]

Meanwhile, the class elimination contests had been in progress; and in early December Johnson announced that Margaret Epley, chosen the outstanding girl debater at Sam Houston the previous year, and Evelyn Lee had won the girls' division after defeating other class opponents as well as the team from the Houston Junior College. A few days later, in a spirited contest

---

[31]Interview with Helen Weinberg, Houston, August 14, 1964.

[32]Houston *Press,* December 10, 1930, p. 1.

presided over by Horace Swale, Houston businessman, with Assistant Principal George Loescher acting as critic judge, Luther E. Jones, Jr., and Gene Latimer were declared the winners over Nat Pacini and Tom Cooksey and so joined Epley and Lee to comprise the Sam Houston team. Arguments in the debate centered on the Interscholastic League topic for the year, "Resolved, that a substitute for trial by jury should be adopted,"[33] and were reported by the Houston *Press* as follows:

The jury system was still standing Wednesday, after staggering groggily Tuesday night at Sam Houston High School through thunderous medleys of brickbats and bouquets.

It was garbed by Sam Houston debaters as a disgrace to the country, and as the safeguard of democracy; as rotten to the core, and as the foundation of justice and mercy.

Nat Pacini and Tom Cooksey resolved, before an interested audience, that the jury system ought to be abolished for a substitute . . . , hurling verbal grenades and citations ranging from Napoleon to the Maples case.

L. E. Jones, who has been selected as the outstanding orator at Sam Houston, and Gene Latimer drove through the barricade while dexterously pasting the jury system together again.[34]

Within six weeks after his arrival, Johnson had selected his team and proceeded to establish for it a training schedule unprecedented in the history of the school. Between early December and the following April his debaters engaged in more than fifty contests, all of them preparatory to the Interscholastic League events to be held in the late spring. This competition began with a series of friendly no-decision debates between Sam Houston and San Jacinto,[35] which was arranged by Johnson and the coach of the rival team, J. P. Barber, and continued with similar contests with the Houston Junior College group. In March, Lee, Epley, Jones, and Latimer, accompanied by Coach Johnson, made an extended tour through Central and South Texas. They engaged teams in Pearsall, where Johnson and the Houston team were

---

[33]Bedicheck, *Educational Competition: The Story of the University Interscholastic League,* 480.

[34]Houston *Press,* December 10, 1930, p. 8.

[35]The outstanding debater on the San Jacinto team was John H. Crooker, Jr., son of a well-known Houston attorney. Crooker was campaign manager for the Kennedy-Johnson ticket in Houston in 1960 and served in Washington on a special assignment from Johnson during the 1964 campaign.

honored by his former students, and also in Carrizo Springs, San Antonio, and San Marcos. The group participated in a total of twelve practice debates. This tour was an innovation in Texas high school debating and earned for Johnson a letter of commendation from Roy Bedicheck, famed Texas naturalist and author, who helped develop the University Interscholastic League and was its director for many years.[36] At the conclusion of the tour Johnson announced that all four members of his team would share equally in the M. E. Foster award, having been selected for the honor by Harvey Harris of the Houston Junior College department of speech.

Already the students and their director had achieved considerable local renown, but their work was just beginning. With the city meet—the first stage in the league program—less than a month away, Jim Winfree, newly elected debate manager who made all of the arrangements for the South Texas tour, declared that fourteen debates still remained on the schedule. Johnson continued to work long hours with his team and again exhibited the talent for getting others to assist him. One colleague, who had no interest in debating or public speaking at all, discovered, after conferring with Lyndon about one of his performers with whom she was having some difficulty, that she had agreed to remain after school to help judge the practice contests; and she was soon chauffeuring members of the team around Houston to help them meet their crowded schedule.[37] With singleminded concentration and enormous drive, Johnson pushed his students to their maximum capacity and managed to fire them with his own determination and enthusiasm. He wanted to win, and so did they. He thought he had the material to do it; so he drove himself and his students and all others he could persuade to assist him toward that one objective.

These efforts were rewarded on the first of April when Sam Houston debaters defeated the boys' team from San Jacinto and the girls' team from Milby before a capacity audience at Taylor School, thus winning the right to represent the city in the county

---

[36]Houston *Press*, March 6, 1931, p. 12. The issue dated December 10, 1930, p. 3, contains the announcement of the projected tour and its itinerary.

[37]Interview with Ellana Ball, Houston, October 24, 1964.

elimination contests two weeks later.[38] The day after the city event, students from all five Houston high schools competed for the literary and forensic championship of the city, the first such contest that had ever been held. Events included all forms of public speaking, in addition to contests in spelling, essay, typing, Latin, and other subjects. Representatives from Sam Houston won either first or second place in every event that they entered; they scored 115 points, 30 more than the nearest rival, San Jacinto. The only disappointment was the defeat of Latimer and Jones by the team they had defeated the day before in the city meet. It was, however, a great occasion for the students and faculty of the downtown school, who welcomed the contestants at a general meeting Friday morning and proudly added six loving cups to their collection of trophies. In presenting the awards, Principal Moyes said:

Sam Houston is indeed proud of the outstanding work of her debaters and public speakers who have won the highest honors possible in competition against the best debaters and public speakers available in any high school in the city. We take great pride in two facts. The winning of first place in boys' debate [in Inter-scholastic League competition] means much more than the winning of one contest. In this case, it represents the winning of honors by two boys who have been named as being two of the best high school debaters ever heard in this city. Credit for the work of these boys, Gene Latimer and L. E. Jones, is due to the splendid work in all lines of public speaking done by L. B. Johnson, who is making a great record in his first year as a teacher in a Houston school.[39]

In addition to the coveted championship trophy, Sam Houston students won the Safford cup given by H. R. Safford and the Kiwanis Club for best performances in forensic events. To receive the award, Moyes, Johnson, members of the debate team, and other Sam Houston students who had won distinction in recent public speaking events (including Helmuth Romberg, Henrietta Daigle, Eleanore Bell, Sam Freeman, and the two outstanding debaters from San Jacinto, John Crooker, Jr., and R. H. Lambert) were invited by the Kiwanis Club to be honored guests at a luncheon in the Rice Hotel on the fifteenth of April.

[38]Houston *Press,* April 2, 1931, p. 3.
[39]Houston *Chronicle,* April 3, 1931, p. 34.

Upon receipt of the cup from President W. L. Cook, Principal Moyes commented that, since the prize was first offered three years ago, enrollment in debate courses at Sam Houston had more than trebled; and he then presented "the man most responsible for the advancement of public speaking at the school, Debate Coach Lyndon B. Johnson, who came to Sam Houston last fall and rapidly built up a debate team that won the city championship."[40]

Three days later new honors came to the young teacher and his students, for in the Interscholastic League District Meet at the Houston Junior College involving teams from Victoria, Fort Bend, Galveston, Matagorda, and Wharton counties, Jones and Latimer defeated Paul Thompson and John W. Brightwell of Rosenberg; and Lee and Epley won over Ruth McFadden and Carol Womack of Goose Creek. These victories insured Sam Houston a place in the state finals at Austin during the first week in May. [41] Excitement among the students, faculty, and parents and in the community continued to increase as these elimination contests progressed. Each series was conducted before large and attentive audiences and attracted as much interest and enthusiasm as athletic play-offs. Indeed, Dorothea Bright, Johnson's cousin, who was a young college student at the time, recalls that they stimulated all the anticipation and thrill then associated with the World Series.[42] As the state meet in Austin approached, and excitement at Sam Houston reached a new peak, the debate director and his team continued to gather materials concerning the jury system and its possible alternatives, to discuss and argue at length all aspects of the subject, and to participate in practice contests.

Finally, the time arrived for the state championship debates among the district winners from all over the state; and the Sam Houston team and its coach left for Austin. The large number of students participating in the various athletic and literary contests, estimated at fifteen hundred, necessitated several rounds of eliminations to determine the final contestants. Margaret Epley and Evelyn Lee were defeated in the first series by Ruth Terrell

[40]Houston *Press,* April 16, 1931, p. 11.

[41]Houston *Post-Dispatch,* April 18, 1931, State News Sec., 6.

[42]Interview with Dorothea Bright Askew, Houston, August 15, 1964.

and Doris Wagner of Victoria; but L. E. Jones and Gene Latimer drew a bye in the first round, won the second, and entered the state finals only to be defeated in a very close contest—the vote was three to two—by Dick Sanders and Warner Evans of Sherman.[43] After so many months of hard and continuous effort and with the state championship within grasp, defeat in the finals was a bitter disappointment for the debaters and their young coach; but it did not diminish the pride of Sam Houston in the team, which had established a remarkable record of achievement and brought new laurels to the school.

Three weeks before the contests in Austin the Houston *Post-Dispatch* had published a long article on the fine performance of Johnson and his debaters and announced that a banquet in their honor was being planned by the students and faculty of Sam Houston, to which former Governor Pat M. Neff of Waco and State Senator Welly K. Hopkins had been invited as principal speakers. The choice of Neff and Hopkins was undoubtedly at Lyndon's suggestion, for the former governor had been a long-time friend of his father, and Hopkins, the youngest member of the Texas Senate, had been materially assisted in winning the senatorial election of 1930 by Lyndon Johnson, who had managed his campaign.

Extensive accounts of the banquet, held at the Lamar Hotel in late May, were carried in all of the Houston newspapers; and accolades were extended to Miss Verna Benton and members of the Tiger Club, sponsors of the event, for bringing together representatives from all of the Sam Houston organizations, delegates from other high schools, school administrators, and city notables to honor Johnson and his debaters. Pat Neff could not attend, but his place was ably filled by Editor M. E. Foster, who, in his comments, cited the "forceful simplicity in Shakespeare and the Bible as fine studies for young people seeking to perfect themselves in the art of public speaking." Senator Hopkins, after paying tribute to the honored guests and to Johnson, spoke on the "world's need of holding to the basic laws of self-government and the true principles of democracy" and praised the

---

[43]Austin *American*, May 7, 1931, p. 1; additional information concerning these debates was furnished by Mr. L. E. Jones, Jr., now a practicing attorney in Corpus Christi. L. E. J. to E. C., November 21, 1964.

inclusion of speech courses in the high school curriculum. After demonstrating to the audience the "speech arts as used in political campaign speeches," he concluded by saying:

There can never be a finer art to which education can devote itself. Some of these young men and young women before me will, within a few years, be sitting in the halls of our legislature, and will win distinction by their ability to sway public opinion gracefully and efficiently by the spoken word.[44]

The awarding of Sam Houston "letters" by Principal Moyes to the championship debaters and to students who had won honors in declamation and extemporaneous speaking brought the occasion to a close. Thus was concluded a remarkably successful year in which, after a period of only seven months, Johnson had brought distinction upon himself and his school. The esteem and affection which he had earned in that brief time were expressed by the student newspaper in a full-page tribute entitled "Who's Who in Sam Houston." Beneath his photograph was the following caption:

Pleasing in personality, indefatigable in his labors, zealous in all his undertakings. Although one of our newest faculty members, he has carved for himself a place in Sam Houston as one of the outstanding teachers.[45]

On the day after the banquet the Houston School Board at its regular meeting reappointed Johnson to the Sam Houston faculty for another year and raised his salary to $1700.00, an income he was able to supplement later in the fall by teaching night school.[46]

Upon returning to Houston in September, 1931, Johnson began the task of rebuilding his debate group around the one remaining member of his championship team, Gene Latimer, the others having graduated in May. He was fortunate in having several students who had had some experience in public speaking; and his star orator of the year before, L. E. Jones, Jr., was a freshman at Rice Institute and thus available to lend a hand.

---

[44]Houston *Post-Dispatch*, May 24, 1931, Sec. 1, p. 10.

[45]*The Printer's Devil* (Houston, Texas), April 10, 1931.

[46]*Board Minutes*, the Houston Independent School District, Book E, 121, 170. George Johnson was also accorded a $100.00 raise, the last he was to receive before the sharp reductions in salary which began to be imposed in 1933.

His assistance was soon needed, for Johnson immediately launched into a schedule even more varied and energetic than that of the previous year. In addition to the class elimination contests through which the new team would be selected, a program was mapped out by Assistant Principal Loescher whereby speakers from Sam Houston would give talks on "timely civic projects" to other classes at the school and to those in the various junior and senior high schools in the city. With the aid of Jones, work on this project was well under way by mid-November.[47]

Later in the month a member of the history faculty, who was also a sponsor of the Sam Houston yearbook, was in the administrative offices on business when a long distance call came for Johnson from Corpus Christi—a call that was to start the young teacher on the road to the presidency. Richard Kleberg, the victor in a recent special election to fill the vacancy in the House of Representatives from the Fourteenth Congressional District, was on the line asking whether Johnson would come to Corpus Christi to discuss the possibility of an appointment as the congressman's private secretary. Helen Weinberg remembers Johnson's reaction:

> He was so excited he didn't know what to say. He said that he would consult with his uncle and call back in a few minutes. When he hung up, he turned to me and said with great excitement, "Mr. Kleberg wants me to be his private secretary. I'll have to go up and tell Uncle George." And I suppose he did, but I was not in the office when he returned the call.[48]

Johnson left Houston almost immediately for Corpus Christi, where he met and talked with Kleberg; and on November 29, 1931, the congressman announced that Johnson had been appointed to the position.[49]

Since Congress was scheduled to convene on the seventh of December, Johnson had little time to conclude his affairs at Sam Houston, assist in finding a replacement, and visit with his family before leaving for Washington; but all of these he managed to do. He applied for a leave of absence, which the school board

[47]Houston *Post-Dispatch*, November 10, 1931, Sec. 1, p. 5; November 15, 1931, Local News Sec., 1.

[48]Interview with Helen Weinberg, Houston, August 14, 1964.

[49]San Antonio *Express*, November 30, 1931, p. 1.

granted in mid-December and continued to extend annually at Johnson's request until 1935.[50] He called his college friend, David Hollis Frazer, also a graduate of Southwest Texas State Teachers College, who was doing graduate work at the University of Colorado, to ask whether he would be interested in the Sam Houston position. Then Johnson visited briefly with his family in San Marcos. Six days after his appointment the Houston *Post-Dispatch* announced that he had arrived in Washington to begin his new duties and that Frazer had been appointed to succeed him at Sam Houston.[51] In reviewing the record which he had established during the brief period that he taught in Houston, the newspaper continued:

> Young Johnson, only 23 years of age in 1930-31, his first year as debate coach at Sam Houston, turned out a winning team which carried off local and district honors in the interscholastic league contests, and placed as runner-up in the state contest in Austin last spring. Himself an orator of much ability, Johnson coached with a contagious enthusiasm which made him a favorite, not only with his own pupils, but with the entire school.[52]

His teaching career had been brief, spanning all of nineteen months, divided roughly between Cotulla and Houston; but it was a distinguished one, memorable to his students and fellow-teachers alike. Into it he poured all of his seemingly inexhaustible energy and desire to succeed and demanded of himself as much as he asked of others, if not more. It would be a commentary upon his performance in the career he was now entering when, upon returning to Sam Houston for a visit several years later, he remarked to a former colleague, "I used to work awfully hard

---

[50]*Board Minutes,* The Houston Independent School District, Book E, 177; Book F, 69, 118, 219. There is no record of any request for leave after 1934 nor any official notice of resignation.

[51]Houston *Post-Dispatch,* December 6, 1931, Society and Club News, 7; interview with Mrs. Roy Dealy, sister of Frazer, Houston, October 23, 1964. Under Frazer's direction, the Sam Houston debaters went to the state finals again in May, 1932, but were eliminated in the first round by teams from Wichita Falls and San Antonio. (The Dallas *Morning News,* May 7, 1932, Sec. 1, p. 4.) Frazer resigned several years later to run, successfully, for the Texas House of Representatives. After a brief interim another Southwest Texas State College graduate, York T. Willbern, was engaged to teach public speaking at Sam Houston. Willbern is currently University Professor at Indiana University and one of the leading authorities in the United States on public administration.

[52]Houston *Post-Dispatch,* December 6, 1931, Society and Club News, 7.

when I was a teacher, but you don't know anything about work until you become a congressman."[53]

It is a long way from Cotulla to Washington, from Sam Houston High School to the White House. For Johnson, the journey required better than thirty years. The events which led him out of the classroom onto the floors of congress and ultimately into the oval office of the presidency began before he had completed his college career.

[53]Interview with Byron Parker, Houston, August 14, 1964.

VIII.

THE YOUNG POLITICIAN

1

JOHNSON CAME BY HIS GREAT INTEREST IN POLITICS QUITE NATurally. His father had been in the Texas legislature and, at the time of his son's appointment to Kleberg's staff, was serving as an inspector in the motor transportation division of the Texas Railroad Commission. His uncle George, though not a professional politician, was vitally interested in public affairs and loved to debate and discuss them with his students as well as with his nephew. Johnson's own political aptitude, enlarged and sharpened by the stimulating discussions of public policy and current events in Professor Greene's course in American government and his own experiences as a college debater, was evident on numerous occasions while he was a student at San Marcos. Johnson's editorials in the college newspaper reflected a deep respect for the Constitution and the law, for representative government and the fundamental rights of all citizens, and for the sacrifices made by countless Americans to protect the principles and traditions of the nation. Frequently hortatory in tone, they admonished the students to strive for higher standards; to practice the virtues of honesty, courtesy, diligence, and self-control; and to make the most of time and present opportunities. Through all of them ran a consistent theme: reasonableness is the safest guide to action and the surest avenue to constructive achievement.

His entrance into professional politics began in 1930 while he was still a senior in college, and after he returned to San Marcos from Cotulla to complete work on his degree. He could scarcely have chosen a more exciting year in which to make his debut. The first of the several major slumps in the stock market, beginning in October, 1929, had precipitated political controversy from the courthouse to the White House. On the national level President Hoover was under increasing attack for his policies or, in the opinion of his opponents, lack of them, in dealing with the depression. Congress was almost evenly divided between Democrats and Republicans and moving slowly toward a deadlock, with keen interest focused upon the outcome of the elections in the fall. In Texas, still overwhelmingly a one-party state despite the fact that its electoral vote had gone to Hoover in 1928, Democrats were slugging it out with each other at all political levels, with the gubernatorial campaign between Mrs. Miriam A. (Ma) Ferguson and Ross Sterling, along with nine other Democratic aspirants, attracting the most attention.

A few fortunate candidates, such as James P. Buchanan, who was running for re-election to the United States Congress from the Tenth Congressional District, and Morris Sheppard, who was campaigning for another term in the Senate, expected little difficulty; but they were exceptions in a year filled with local, state, and national controversy over the economic situation, the perennial issue of prohibition, and the usual sharp division over local issues. Johnson's interest was focused upon the contests in his own county and district rather than those on the state level; and, like hundreds of other citizens, he attended various local political rallies held during the campaign. These rallies, to which all candidates were invited and given the opportunity to speak, were common at the time and usually well attended. Such a meeting occurred on the lawn of the courthouse in San Marcos on July 25, 1930; and all district, county, and precinct candidates were invited. Oren Cliett, the Democratic County Chairman, expected it to be the largest political meeting ever held in Hays County; and he urged all citizens to attend, "especially the ladies."[1] A similar rally was held early in the campaign at Henly, a small community near the Hays-Blanco county line. Welly K. Hopkins, later to be one of the principal speakers at the banquet in Houston honoring Johnson and his debate team, was present and recalled the occasion as follows:

This was an annual affair attended by people from all the surrounding areas, and it was traditional for State candidates, as well as those on the district and local levels, to appear either in person or through some spokesman in behalf of their candidacies. The meeting was held in a grove of live oak trees, an all-day "picnic on the grounds" affair typical of that day and thoroughly representative of the politics of the time.[2]

Hopkins had good reason to be there. A member of the Texas House of Representatives from Gonzales, a small community thirty miles east of San Antonio, he had decided, upon the announcement of State Senator Alvin J. Wirtz of Seguin that he would not seek re-election, to run for the Texas Senate from the Nineteenth State Senatorial District. This district comprised six counties, including Blanco, the traditional home of the Johnsons, and Hays, where Lyndon and his family were then residing while he and his sisters were in college. Early in his campaign against Tom Gambrell, a well-known lawyer from Lockhart, Hopkins discussed his candidacy with the influential and politically experienced men throughout the district, including Lyndon's father,

---

[1]San Marcos *Record,* July 25, 1930.

[2]Welly K. Hopkins to E. C., December 3, 1964.

Sam Johnson, whose endorsement he received. Thenceforth, wherever Hopkins campaigned, especially in Hays and Blanco counties where he was less strong, he sought out the elder Johnson's friends and acquaintances and solicited their support. Taking advantage of every opportunity to appear before the electorate, he was present at the Henly political rally and recalls that

The speaker's stand was a country wagon with the tail gate let down, each candidate in turn being invited by the master of ceremonies to climb up on the end of the wagon and, after a brief introduction, to proclaim his virtues and abilities to the assembled voters. There were several hundred people present that day, scattered in and around the grove of trees, under one of which the speaker's wagon was placed. In mid-afternoon, my turn having arrived, I was introduced and proceeded to show cause why I should receive the Democratic nomination over my opponent, an attorney of Lockhart, Caldwell County, by the name of Tom Gambrell.[3]

After he finished his speech and returned to the crowd to continue electioneering on an individual basis, Hopkins heard the master of ceremonies call out the name of former Governor Pat Neff, who had been appointed to the Texas Railroad Commission and was seeking election. When no one responded to several calls and the chairman was "in the act of declaring a default," Hopkins heard a "loud, youthful voice yell out, 'I will make a speech for Pat Neff,' and with the voice there quickly emerged from the crowd a tall, slender, bright-eyed, brunette young man who immediately pushed his way forward and climbed up on the tail gate." After being introduced as "Lyndon, Sam Johnson's boy," he proceeded to make "an enthusiastic, arm-swinging defense of Neff as governor and as railroad commissioner, proclaiming his virtues and abilities as being in every way superior to those of his opponent—a completely extemporaneous and spontaneous speech of approximately ten to fifteen minutes, all in the style typical of the customs of the region and the politics of the time." The speech was roundly applauded; and when Johnson had rejoined the crowd, Hopkins made his way to him, introduced himself, and said, "Lyndon, why did you volunteer this speech for Pat Neff?" Johnson replied, in sub-

---

[3]*Ibid.*

stance, "I couldn't let it go by default. Pat Neff once gave my daddy a job and I couldn't let him down."[4]

Hopkins, who was impressed with young Johnson's sense of loyalty and his willingness to speak up in behalf of the candidacy of his father's friend, asked him to be his campaign manager. Lyndon readily accepted the offer. From that moment until the election in late July, Hopkins and Johnson worked closely together, with Lyndon "calling the shots," particularly in Blanco, Hays, and Comal counties where he had family and school connections. He effectively exploited the two most explosive issues of the campaign, the Ku Klux Klan and prohibition, both of which Hopkins opposed. Johnson also set up an "organization of sorts" into which his family and friends were drawn. This group distributed campaign literature, saw to it that Hopkins's speeches were well attended, and "besieged their families and friends to support me actively and acted as a vocal, effective cheering section at the larger meetings."[5]

The young campaign manager, still a college student, solicited funds and votes and arranged for political advertisements in the various county newspapers. The burden of Johnson's argument was that, since the Nineteenth District had never been represented in the Texas Senate by a native of Gonzales County, Hopkins, who was eminently qualified, ought to be elected.[6] In the closing days of the campaign Lyndon planned two large political rallies, one at New Braunfels and the other at San Marcos. These efforts were rewarded in late July when Hopkins won the Democratic primary by more than two thousand votes, and lost only Caldwell and Hays counties by slender margins.[7] This victory assured Hopkins of a seat in the Texas Senate, although he would face token Republican opposition in November at the general election. For all practical purposes the campaign was over, and the new senator and his campaign manager made plans to celebrate their successful efforts at the first opportunity. "On the same evening that Lyndon received his diploma at graduation exercises in August," Hopkins recalls, "we held a sort of victory

[4]*Ibid.*

[5]*Ibid.*

[6]San Marcos *Record,* July 18, 1930.

[7]*Ibid.,* August 1, 1930.

party, and later we took a brief vacation together on an automobile trip to Monterey [Mexico]."[8]

Upon their return from this trip, Hopkins went on to Gonzales to prepare for the November election and the coming session of the Texas legislature; and Lyndon made plans to go to Pearsall to teach, no opening in the Houston school system having developed. Their friendship, which had only recently begun but was cemented during the arduous days of the summer campaign, continued after Lyndon left Pearsall in late October to begin his duties at Sam Houston High School. The following May, Hopkins and Johnson again held "a sort of victory party"—this time in Houston—when the young senator joined with others to honor his former campaign manager for his outstanding performance as teacher of public speaking and director of debate.[9]

2

During Lyndon Johnson's youth, his hometown of Johnson City, located in the Fourteenth Congressional District which included eleven counties stretching all the way from his own Blanco in Central Texas to Nueces on the Gulf, had been represented by the popular and able Republican congressman from Seguin, Harry M. Wurzbach. Swept into office by the Republican landslide of 1920, he was re-elected for six consecutive terms despite the opposition of the regular Republican organization, headed by National Committeeman R. B. Creager of Brownsville, and the repeated efforts of Democrats to unseat him. A man widely respected, with a large personal following, Wurzbach had the distinction of being the only Republican in the Texas congressional delegation, the third man of his party to represent.the state since its admission to the Union in 1846, and the only one to be elected to congress for more than two terms.[10]

When he entered Santa Rosa Infirmary in San Antonio for an abdominal operation in early November, 1931, his vote in the House of Representatives was vital, for that body was almost evenly divided between the two major parties, with the candi-

[8]W. K. Hopkins to E. C., December 3, 1964.
[9]Houston *Post-Dispatch*, May 24, 1931, Sec. 1, p. 10.
[10]Dallas *Morning News*, November 7, 1931, pp. 1, 7.

dacy of John Nance Garner of Texas for the speakership hanging in the balance.[11] Of great importance to the Seguin-San Antonio region was the fact that Wurzbach had been a very effective member of the House Military Affairs Committee, whose policies and decisions were of vital concern to the many military establishments around San Antonio. The congressman survived the operation and was improving steadily, much to the relief of his many constituents and friends; then, on the third day, his condition worsened, an embolus formed, and within six hours he was dead.[12]

Wurzbach's sudden and unexpected death shocked and grieved his numerous associates and supporters and his friends throughout the state, and it electrified the political scene locally and nationally. Both in the district and in Washington speculation immediately developed concerning his successor. It was generally believed that the Democrats would fill the vacancy, in which case control of the House and the election of Garner would be assured. But the national leaders of the party were uneasy, since Texas laws required that the governor call a special election, the winner to be determined by a plurality vote. A single Republican running against several Democrats might have a reasonably good chance of victory; and the hopes of the Grand Old Party were buoyed when Carl Wright Johnson, Democrat from San Antonio, entered the race, as rumors circulated that several others were on the verge of announcing their candidacies. The Republicans were hampered, however, by internal dissension and the absence of a candidate with the personal appeal and popular following of Wurzbach, whose control of the District seat was truly a Texas political anomaly.

On November 13, one week after the death of Wurzbach, Governor Ross Sterling announced that the special election to fill the late congressman's position would be held on November 24, eleven days thence.[13] During the two and one-half weeks that

---

[11]The division was as follows: Democrats—217; Republicans—215; Farmer-Laborite—1; vacancies—2. Republican control of the House, as well as the Senate, had been weakened seriously by adverse political returns in the 1930 election and the death of several national legislators.

[12]Dallas *Morning News*, November 7, 1931, Sec. 1, p. 1.

[13]Dallas *Morning News*, November 14, 1931, Sec. 1, p. 1. There is no mention of this election in J. Evetts Haley's campaign tract, *A Texan Looks at Lyndon: A*

intervened between Wurzbach's death and the selection of a successor, ten candidates entered the race, two of whom withdrew in the last days of the campaign, leaving seven Democrats and one Republican to fight it out. This situation further alarmed the Democratic leadership, which appealed to party members several times during the race to unite behind one candidate—any of the seven—to insure victory. Similar efforts were made locally, all to no avail.[14] When the Republicans achieved some degree of unanimity between the Creager and the anti-Creager forces in support of C. W. Anderson, the late congressman's personal attorney and close friend, Washington Democrats became even more anxious; but they continued to be assured by those close to the scene that a Democratic victory was virtually certain.[15]

Throughout the brief but intensive campaign, only three of the candidates were considered serious contenders for the position: Anderson and two Democrats, Carl W. Johnson of San Antonio, who had the backing of the "city-county ring," which, according to the Dallas *Morning News*, was "a favorable asset in itself,"[16] and Richard Kleberg, lawyer and rancher from Corpus Christi and son of Robert J. Kleberg, one of the owners of the famed King Ranch. Outside of Republican circles, Anderson was conceded little chance of victory in a district predominantly Democratic, and attention was focused upon the contest between Carl Johnson and Kleberg. Each man sought support in the other's strongest area, Johnson by promising voters in the Corpus Christi region that he would strongly support federal assistance in developing its port facilities, Kleberg by being equally solicitous of San Antonio's vital stake in its military establishments. A central issue in the campaign was the prohibition question, with both men supporting some modification of

Study in Illegitimate Power (Canyon, Texas, 1964). Liberty Lobby's *LBJ: A Political Biography* (Washington, D. C., 1964) mentions it but lists Richard Kleberg's opponent as Thurmond Barrett, which is an error. Barrett ran against Kleberg in the Democratic primary in July, 1932, in which the latter was renominated. (San Antonio *Express*, July 24, 1932, p. 1; July 25, 1932, p. 1.)

[14]San Antonio *Express*, November 19, 1931, pp. 1, 2; November 20, 1931, p. 11.

[15]Dallas *Morning News*, November 8, 1931, Sec. 1, p. 3; November 15, 1931, Sec. 1, p. 3; November 17, 1931, Sec. 1, p. 3; November 19, 1931, Sec. 1, p. 3; November 19, 1931, Sec. 2, p. 8; November 29, 1931, Sec. 1, pp. 1, 7.

[16]Dallas *Morning News*, November 28, 1931, Sec. 1, p. 7.

the laws respecting its enforcement, although Carl Johnson had earlier stated in his platform that he believed in "upholding the Constitution of the United States and in law enforcement."[17] Both candidates supported states' rights and asserted that the federal government had overstepped the bounds of its authority in local and state matters, and Johnson wooed the support of veterans by endorsing immediate payment at face value of the soldiers' bonus.[18]

Carl Johnson's greatest strength lay in Bexar County, where he had the support of the "city machine" and the San Antonio Labor Council as well as the endorsement of numerous friends and associates.[19] His chances were weakened, however, by the decision of the Democratic caucus, representing seven of the eleven counties, to support Kleberg; and by the strong opposition of the Citizens' League, a reform organization led by Maury Maverick, John Boyle, and W. A. Wurzbach, brother of the late Republican congressman. Established several years earlier for the purpose of wresting control of San Antonio and Bexar County from the "city-county machine," the League had been unsuccessful prior to 1930 in its efforts to displace the "courthouse" candidates.[20] In the Democratic primary elections of that year, however, League nominees were swept into the offices of district attorney, county attorney, county judge, county tax collector, and sheriff, although they failed in their bid to win control of the city government.[21] The long and persistent opposition of the Citizens' League to "machine candidates" and its endorsement of Kleberg brought a lament from Paul Steffler of San Antonio, an aide of Carl Johnson, who told more than one thousand city employees that

Whatever opposition had developed in San Antonio toward Johnson was the result of the same forces which had always opposed the city administration; . . . they would have opposed any candidate which Mayor C. M. Chambers and other city officials had endorsed. They

---

[17]San Antonio *Express,* November 18, 1931, p. 22.

[18]*Ibid.,* November 19, 1931, p. 2.

[19]*Ibid.,* November 21, 1931, p. 7; Dallas *Morning News,* November 21, 1931, Sec. 1, p. 3.

[20]Dallas *Morning News,* July 9, 1930, Sec. 1, p. 12.

[21]Dallas *Morning News,* July 28, 1930, Sec. 1, p. 2.

have not been able to find anything to say against Carl Wright Johnson and so they are just opposing him on general principles because the city administration is for him.[22]

In other words, bitter rivalry between the "machine" and the Citizens' League was endemic: it prevailed in city and county politics, in the special election of 1931 to choose a congressman, and again in the regular biennial elections of 1932.

Kleberg's strength lay in his own county of Nueces, other areas outside of Bexar, and among the voters of German and Latin descent, whose languages he spoke. When he appeared before some two thousand Latin-Americans in San Antonio, his campaign manager, Roy Miller, former mayor of Corpus Christi and public relations officer for the Texas Gulf Sulphur Company, introduced him as "a cowboy who understands and sympathizes with the Mexican-American people of Southwest Texas," a number of whom worked diligently for him throughout the campaign.[23] Among Kleberg's numerous supporters who made speeches for him was State Senator Welly K. Hopkins, who, on the last day before the election, reminded the voters of Seguin of the "patriotic achievements of the Kleberg family in Texas from the Battle of San Jacinto to the present day."[24]

These various efforts were handsomely rewarded on November 25, for the election returns revealed that Kleberg had carried all but two of the eleven counties in the district, his own by a margin of ten to one. Coming into Bexar County with a lead of more than ten thousand votes, a greater majority than any candidate had ever achieved, Kleberg held a margin that Johnson was unable to overcome and was elected.[25]

The State Canvassing Board certified his victory on November 30, in time for him to attend the Democratic organizational caucus in Washington on December 5, two days prior to the opening of the session. Kleberg's victory was of national signifi-

---

[22]San Antonio *Express*, November 21, 1931, p. 7. For a report on the endorsement of Kleberg by the Democratic caucus, see the Dallas *Morning News*, November 17, 1931, Sec. 1, p. 3.

[23]San Antonio *Express*, November 21, 1931, p. 7.

[24]*Ibid.*, November 24, 1931, pp. 1, 6.

[25]Dallas *Morning News*, November 26, 1931, Sec. 1, p. 1. The final tally was Kleberg: 19,038; Johnson: 13,945; Anderson: 5,759. In Bexar County, Johnson: 12,970; Kleberg: 8,476; Anderson: 4,097. Outside of Bexar County, Johnson received only 975 votes. *1930 Election Register: State and County Officials*, 381. Secretary of State, Austin, Texas.

cance, for it insured Democratic control of the House and the election of John Nance Garner as the new speaker midway in the administration of President Herbert Hoover.[26]

Throughout this campaign Lyndon Johnson was in Houston teaching his classes in public speaking and arranging for the inter-class contests which would determine the membership of his debate team. His friend Senator Welly Hopkins, however, had conceived other plans for him which he immediately put into execution. As mentioned above, Hopkins had campaigned actively for Kleberg by making speeches in his behalf and by working at his headquarters in the Gunter Hotel in San Antonio during the last week of the campaign.[27] Hopkins recalls the subsequent events as follows:

> Immediately after Kleberg's election, I recommended to him that he take Lyndon to Washington as his private secretary. To help accomplish this, I made a special trip to Houston (where Lyndon was then teaching) to talk with him and then paid a call on Roy Miller, now deceased (a close friend and advisor as well as campaign manager for Kleberg), outlining to him Lyndon's capabilities and why I thought Kleberg would benefit in having a private secretary of Lyndon's type. Roy listened carefully and, although he had never met Lyndon, accepted him on my recommendation and agreed to arrange an interview with Kleberg.[28]

It was shortly thereafter that Johnson received the telephone call from Corpus Christi (referred to earlier), which invited him to talk to Kleberg about the possibility of appointment to the congressman's staff. After consulting with his Uncle George and returning the call, Johnson left to go to Corpus Christi for an interview. Hopkins continued:

> Within a day or two afterward, I recall Lyndon and his father driving by my home in Gonzales to tell me that he was en route to Corpus Christi in response to a call from Kleberg, who had told him of my interest. That night Lyndon called me to announce enthusiastically that he had received the appointment, was resigning as debate coach at Sam Houston High School, and would be leaving shortly for Washington.[29]

---

[26]The House lineup was now Democrats: 218; Republicans: 214; Farmer-Laborite: 1; vacancies: 2.

[27]W. K. Hopkins to E. C., December 3, 1964.

[28]*Ibid.*

[29]*Ibid.*

Hurriedly putting his affairs in Houston in order, Johnson left with Kleberg in early December, 1931, to assume his new duties. After almost eight months in Washington, Johnson returned with the congressman in July, 1932, to assist him in his bid for re-election in the Democratic primary against Thurmond Barrett. In this election Kleberg did even better than he had done in the previous year, winning every county in the district except Blanco—ironically--the family home of his private secretary. And he came within a very narrow margin of sweeping Bexar, the home county of his opponent, by a clear majority.[30] The Citizens' League did equally well, continuing its domination of the county which it had established the year before, by sweeping its candidates into all offices except that of district clerk.[31]

Remaining with Kleberg until 1935, Johnson was appointed State Director of the National Youth Administration of Texas, a position he continued to hold until 1937. He resigned in that year to run for the House of Representatives from the Tenth Congressional District.[32] In a special election necessitated by the death of James P. Buchanan, Johnson was elected from a field of ten candidates on April 10, 1937. Four years later, in 1941, in another special election to fill the senatorial seat of Morris Sheppard, Lyndon Johnson suffered one of the few setbacks of his political life, being defeated by W. Lee (Pappy) O'Daniel. Continuing to occupy his place in the House of Representatives, he tried again for the Senate in 1948, this time against former Governor Coke Stevenson, whom he beat in the second primary by the slim margin of 87 out of just under one million votes. Since then his career has been characterized by extraordinary political ability and fortuitous circumstances. He became senate majority leader in 1955, vice-president in 1961, and president upon the tragic assassination of John Fitzgerald Kennedy on November 22, 1963, in Dallas, Texas.

---

[30]San Antonio *Express*, July 25, 1932, p. 1. Almost complete returns gave Kleberg: 28,169; Barrett: 19,516; Britt: 2,794; Maloney: 568. In Bexar County: Kleberg: 13,811; Barrett: 11,857; Britt: 2,041; Maloney: 382.

[31]*Ibid.*

[32]This district was created in 1933 when the Texas legislature reapportioned the state on the basis of the 1930 census. It comprised ten counties in central Texas, including two formerly in Kleberg's district (Blanco and Lee).

IX.

". . . THE LAND WHERE I WAS BORN"

LYNDON BAINES JOHNSON'S EMINENTLY SUCCESSFUL CAREER AS a political leader, climaxed by his sweeping victory in the presidential election of 1964, reflects in many significant ways the influence of his formative years which began in the rug-

« 174 »

gedly beautiful and spacious land of Central Texas. Better than anyone else, he has described the area which nurtured him and his forbears and to which he has constantly returned for sustenance and renewal:

It was once a barren land. The angular hills were covered with scrub cedar and a few live oaks. Little would grow in the harsh caliche soil. And each spring the Pedernales River would flood the valley. But men came and worked and endured and built.[1]

His grandparents and mother and father were among those who came and built and converted the inhospitable land into one "abundant with fruit, cattle, goats and sheep" with "pleasant homes and lakes." Here he was born, and here he grew to young manhood under the solicitous care of parents for whom he held a deep affection.

Johnson's early years were not unlike those of thousands of other young Americans who would later elect him to the highest office in the nation; and from the beginning, the influence of his parents was a dominant factor in his life. His mother taught him to read at an early age, aroused his interest in public speaking and debate, and encouraged him to attain the highest goals his talents would allow. A beautiful and intelligent woman, she was to affect the course of her son's career in numerous imperceptible ways; and in an unsolicited editorial which appeared in the local newspaper while Lyndon was still in college, he paid tribute to all mothers, but most particularly to his own:

. . . where can there be found words to describe one's mother? What adjectives can portray her infinite patience, her unfailing tenderness, her loving care, her amazing self-sacrifice, her wonderful understanding, her intense loyalty?

The affection of friends, sweethearts, brothers, sisters, of all loved ones may be estranged but mother's love abides to the end. Disaster, disgrace, despair and death do not affect the love a mother feels for her child save to add to it compassion and tenderness. There is no love on earth comparable to that of mother. Our best description of it is that of all types of earthly love, it most nearly approaches the divine.

.   .   .   .   .

. . . Our minds acknowledge the great debt mankind owes to mothers.

[1] "Message to the Congress on the State of the Union," New York *Times*, January 6, 1965, Sec. 1, p. 16.

Our hearts declare its truth. Let us today make our lives living tributes and fitting memorials to the splendid characters who have proven the most potent and vital force for good in the world—the mothers of men.[2]

His father introduced him to the exciting world of politics by taking him on campaign trips while the elder Johnson was running for a seat in the Texas House of Representatives between 1918 and 1922. Occasional visits to Austin while the legislature was in session further aroused his interest, and the years at Southwest Texas State College in San Marcos provided an opportunity for the young student from Johnson City to initiate the development of an extraordinary political talent. That he should major in American history, minor in government and the social sciences, and become an able college debater and journalist whose editorials reflected a broad and unusually mature appreciation of history as well as current problems followed naturally from his earlier training and experience; and his energetic participation in a great variety of college activities reflected the lively interest manifested by his parents in community and state affairs.

The Johnsons during Lyndon's early years were neither richer nor poorer than the average Central Texas farm family which had to wrest a living from the rocky, often drought-stricken land; and the recollections of those difficult years have appeared frequently in the speeches of the President and have undoubtedly influenced the development of his anti-poverty program. His concern for the economically depressed in a land rich in resources and opportunities was reinforced by his experiences during the Great Depression. His formal political career, foreshadowed by his energetic involvement in college politics, began in 1930; by the time he arrived in Washington in 1931 as Congressman Kleberg's private secretary, the nation was plagued by serious economic stagnation. During his early years in the nation's capitol, he observed the efforts of the Hoover administration and later those of Franklin D. Roosevelt to ease the massive distress which the depression produced; he became an ardent supporter of the New Deal and a life-long admirer of Roosevelt.

---

[2]"To Our Mothers," San Marcos *Record*, May 9, 1930.

Franklin Delano Roosevelt

In a speech delivered at the inauguration of James H. McCrocklin as president of Southwest Texas State College in November, 1964, Johnson referred to Roosevelt as "a great president, a fearless leader, a man who preserved the Republic in the most challenging period, who talked to me about the third of our land that was ill-fed, ill-clad, and ill-housed, and . . . sought to do something about it."[3] When Roosevelt appointed him director of the National Youth Administration program in Texas, Johnson learned at first-hand the ravaging effects of the depression on young people, an intimation of which he had experienced in Cotulla. Faced with the task of finding employment for hundreds of college students who were being forced out of school in search of jobs which did not exist, he quickly set up an office in the old Littlefield building in Austin and enlisted the aid of Sherman Birdwell, Willard Deason, and Jesse Kellam, all friends from his college days, whom he constantly admonished: "Put them to work, get them in school." Johnson found jobs for nearly 30,000 young people, some of whom learned trades they were to follow the rest of their lives, others earning enough to complete their college careers.[4]

As head of the Texas NYA, young Johnson helped implement the New Deal in his own state; and a part of Roosevelt's vision of a better, more prosperous America became his own. To a remarkable degree his domestic policies are an extension, as Richard Rovere has observed, of the Rooseveltian conception. "The Great Society is an attempt," he wrote, "to codify the New Deal's vision of a good society,"[5] the chief difference being that the Johnson program is an effort to achieve economic and social justice in an age of abundance rather than during one of scarcity and depression.

Johnson's deep conviction that the only escape from the grinding treadmill of poverty and its related ills is education, and his vigorous support of measures to enlarge educational opportunities for the poor and underprivileged again reflect his own ex-

[3]New York *Times*, December 1, 1964, p. 18.

[4]New York *Times*, December 1, 1964, p. 18; Austin *American*, November 25, 1963, p. 1; San Marcos *Record*, April 15, 1965, p. 8.

[5]Richard Rovere, "A Man for This Age, Too," New York *Times Magazine*, April 6, 1965, p. 118.

periences during the formative years. In a speech given in April, 1965, at the dedication of the Camp Gary Job Corps Training Center in San Marcos, one of the first to be established under the Economic Opportunity Act approved by the congress in August, 1964, the president told the trainees that he, too, had once faced the choice of "being a dropout for life, or striving to be something more." The president continued: "I was a dropout from 1924 to 1926. I worked for a dollar a day. I went to California seeking my fortune and almost starved to death before I got back to Texas. But whatever has come to me, the time spent in this cordial city studying and learning did make some little difference. And I hope that it's the same for you."[6]

Johnson was not actually a dropout, but a high school graduate for whom the lure of immediate employment was more appealing than the pursuit of a college degree. His own experience as an unskilled worker convinced him, however, that further education, which his parents had earnestly urged upon him, was essential; and his decision to enter the state college at San Marcos was another turning point in his career. There he came under the influence of President C. E. Evans, who befriended him and provided sufficient employment to keep him in school; Professors H. M. Greene and M. L. Arnold, who quickened his interest in politics and history; and other faculty and townspeople who became warm and lasting friends. During his college career he developed a keen respect for education and the teaching profession. This attitude was reflected at the time in the many editorials which he wrote for the college newspaper, later in his brief but successful tenure as a teacher in Cotulla and Houston, in his work as NYA director in Texas, and most significantly in his successful guidance through congress of the administration's historic federal aid-to-education bill. The latter measure, the first of its kind to achieve congressional approval after nineteen years of effort, provides, in the president's opinion, the essential foundation upon which the Great Society can be built. It was typical of this complex yet sentimental man that he should sign it into law in the yard of the former "Junction School," about two miles down the Pedernales River from the Texas

---

[6]San Marcos *Record,* April 15, 1965, p. 8.

White House, where he began his own formal education. Invited to witness the ceremony were his classmates of Johnson City, some of his former students and colleagues from Cotulla and Houston, and his first-grade teacher, Miss Kate Deadrich, who was flown from California for the event.[7]

In one area of public policy, that of civil rights, the president has gone far beyond the activities of Franklin Roosevelt; and while it is difficult to estimate the extent to which his early experiences may have influenced his present attitudes, he has attested that such an influence did exist. In his now-famous speech on voting rights, delivered to a joint session of the congress in March, 1965, he commented upon his experience in Cotulla and the plight of his students whom he described as poor, frequently hungry, and the innocent victims of prejudice:

I often walked home late in the afternoon, wishing there was more that I could do. Somehow you never forget what poverty and hatred can do when you see its scars on the hopeful face of a young child. I never thought then, in 1928, that I would be standing here in 1965. It never even occurred to me in my fondest dreams that I might have the chance to help the sons and daughters of those students, and to help people like them all over the country. But now I do have that chance. And I'll let you in on a secret —I mean to use it.[8]

Throughout his career Johnson has exhibited characteristics and singular abilities which he first manifested as a school boy, college student, and teacher. Restless and enormously energetic, he possessed an almost over-powering drive, great ambition, a strong commitment to the task at hand, and qualities of aggressive leadership which inspired many of his associates. His approach to problems was imaginative as well as positive, and he exhibited an extraordinary talent for persuading his colleagues to assist him in the search for practical solutions. An indefatigable worker, he was impatient with anything less than top performance by his associates; but he never demanded of them more than he was willing to do himself. His political acumen, aroused by his father and sharpened by his activities as a student, was clearly evidenced in his successful management of Welly K. Hopkins's campaign in

---

[7]Wray Weddell, Jr., Austin *American*, April 12, 1965, pp. 1, 6.

[8]*Time*, March 26, 1965, p. 21.

1930 and his own spectacular career in national politics which began later in the decade.

A man of many parts who combines an almost baffling complexity with a disarming simplicity and warmth of sentiment, which to the uninitiated seems perilously close to sentimentality, Lyndon Johnson is pre-eminently the product of the people and the land from which he sprang. And it is to these that he returns as often as his responsibilities allow. More than any other national leader of recent memory, his identity is rooted in the attachments and the experiences of his early years for which he feels an unrestrained and affectionate loyalty. He remarked in his State of the Union address in January, 1965: "A president's hardest task is not to do what is right, but to know what is right. Yet the presidency brings no special gift of prophecy or foresight. You take an oath, step into an office, and must help guide a great democracy. The answer was waiting for me in the land where I was born."[9]

---

[9]New York *Times*, January 5, 1965, Sec. 1, p. 16.

Index

« 183 »

Romberg, Helmuth, 155
Roosevelt, Franklin Delano, 34, 48, 176, 177, 178, 180
Roth, Fenner, 109, 111
Rountree, Louis, 53
Rovere, Richard, 178
Ruth, George Herman, 139
Sam Houston Normal School, 69
Sam Houston Senior High School, 145-159, 167
Sandburg, Carl, 86
Sanders, Dick, 157
San Jacinto High School, 147, 152, 154, 155
San Marcos, Texas, 14, 24, 45, 47, 54, 66, 67-111, 144, 176
San Saba Mission, 7
Santa Anna, 124
Sauer, Emil, 33
Sessom, Mike, 11
Sewell, S. M., 84, 92
Shands, Henry, 92, 105
Sheppard, Morris, 163, 173
Shipp family, 23
Silk, George, 2
Skinner, Cornelia Otis, 86
Smith, Alfred E., 138, 139
Smith, Lon, 48
Smith, H. R., 41
Spampinato, Michael, 151
Spaulding, Tiny, 56
Speck, Henry Eli, 86, 91, 130
Speer, John, 12, 14, 17
Spinn, Dick, 110
Socrates, 113
Solms-Braunfels, Prince Carl, 9
Southwestern University, 78
Southwest Texas State College, 47, 59, 66, 67-136, 143, 176, 178
Stetson-hat era, 45
Stevenson, B., 65
Stevenson, Coke, 173
Stevenson, W., 65
Steffler, Paul, 170
Sterling, Ross, 168
St. Mary's University, 85
Stonewall, Texas, 10, 24, 49, 50, 54
Strahan, O. W., 81, 84, 91, 103, 104
Stribling, C., 65
Stubbs, Ben Jack, 34
Stubbs, N. T., 34
Stucken, Alfred Vander, 33
Sul Ross State College, 81

Sutton, W. A., 86
Swale, Horace, 153
Talbott, Edward, 143
Tampke, R. A., 91
Taylor, Sue, 81
Terrell Election Law, 26
Terrell, Ruth, 156
Texas Association of Colleges and Universities, 76
Texas Good Roads Association, 29
Texas Interscholastic League, 65, 142, 143, 153-156
Texas Railroad Commission, 43-44, 162, 165
Thomas, Gates, 81, 92
Thompson, Paul, 156
Thoreau, Henry David, 92
Throckmorton, J. W., 30
Trenckman, W. A., 41
University of Pennsylvania, 76
University of Texas, 69, 73, 80
Votaw, David, 90
Wagner, A. J., 34
Wagner, Doris, 157
Wahrmund, Lorlie, 33
Walch, Felix J., 41
Wallace, S. W., 28
Waters-Pearce Oil Company, 29
Watson, John M., 20
Webb, Walter P., 5
Weinberg, Helen, 159
Welhausen Ward School, 141-145
White Oak School, 23
Whitesides, Vernon, 98, 105, 107, 108
White Stars, 105ff.
Wildenthal, Bryan, 81, 92, 130
Wiley, E. O., 81, 91
Williams Drug Store, 82
Williams, Roger, 113
Wilson, Woodrow, 34, 39, 48, 119, 128
Winfree, Jim, 154
Winters, William, 11
Wirtz, Alvin J., 164
Withers Opera House, 44, 46
Woods, Wilton, 97, 105, 108
Woodson, W. I., 92
Womack, Carol, 156
Waugh, Gene Barnwell, 53, 56, 57
Wright, L. N., 81, 92
Wright, W. A., 26, 28
Wurzbach, Harry M., 167-169
Wurzbach, W. A., 170
Yarborough, Ralph W., 57
Zodiac, 9